Reclaiming Her Story

Reclaiming Her Story

THE WITNESS OF WOMEN IN THE OLD TESTAMENT

by
Jon L. Berquist

Wipf & Stock
PUBLISHERS
Eugene, Oregon

Wipf and Stock Publishers
199 W 8th Ave, Suite 3
Eugene, OR 97401

Reclaiming Her Story
The Witness of Women in the Old Testament
By Berquist, Jon L.
Copyright©1992 by Berquist, Jon L.
ISBN: 1-59752-510-3
Publication date: 1/9/2006
Previously published by Chalice Press, 1992

Dedication

For the participants in
Phillips Graduate Seminary's course
on women in the Old Testament
during spring 1991,
who shared their lives
with me as we searched
to reclaim these
ancient stories
of faith.

Acknowledgments

Many of the insights in this book began as discussion in my class on women in the Old Testament at Phillips Graduate Seminary, Tulsa, Oklahoma, in the spring of 1991. I learned an amazing amount from these women and men who shared themselves in that class. Their perspectives and their honest, sensitive grappling with these delicate, thorny issues made this book possible. My special thanks go to the five students who helped in planning the class sessions: Jill Clupper, Diana Crawford, Mary Lou Martin, Myrna Peterson, and Linda Pope.

I must also mention several examples of women of faith who have shaped my thoughts and feelings. In early years, my grandmother, Elsie Entrekin, and my mother, Mary Beth Berquist, were most influential. Edith Ackerman, an elder at First Christian Church (Disciples of Christ), Ventura, California, taught me so much. More recently, Lauren Odell-Scott was my pastor and close friend at Eastwood Christian Church (Disciples of Christ), Nashville, Tennessee; I see her still as the fulfillment of what can be. Now, many of my students are adding themselves to this list of influence. Of that group, I owe special thanks to Leslie Penrose for her challenge to write this book. Her challenge came not only in her words, but also in her own commitments and risks to live her faith and ministry.

I am especially indebted to Nancy and Frank Kouns for their gracious provision of quiet space to enable the writing of these pages. I also was privileged to share parts of these thoughts during Nancy's ordination service.

Many churches have been kind to listen to my retellings of these women's stories, and their encouragement and debate have been most helpful in improving this material. Among these are Harvard Avenue Christian Church (Disciples of Christ), East Side Christian Church (Disciples of Christ), and Memorial Drive United Methodist Church, all of Tulsa, as well as Jenks United Methodist Church, of Jenks, Oklahoma. Additionally, Peggy Dean offered comments full of insightful critique and pushed me to reconsider several points.

My deepest appreciation goes to David Polk, the editor of Chalice Press, for his willingness to undertake this project despite its multiple unorthodoxies. His courageous enabling gave me the energy to place these words on their pages.

During the times of writing and editing this book, my best friend kept me going when I questioned the whole project. I give thanks to God for her, in part because she not only read the manuscript, but believed it. When she told me that these pages echoed her own life, she gave me the highest compliment possible, for her life has been an untold treasure.

Contents

Preface

Why should a man write a book about the women of the Old Testament?

It's a good question, and I've struggled with that throughout my work on this project.

The answer takes the form of a conviction and a compulsion. The first of these is my conviction that the Bible's stories are stories for all people, because they work together to form faith. A faith that relies only on *part* of the Bible is not a full faith, no matter what part one chooses. In the context of the Old Testament's women, I am convinced that these stories are for everyone. The stories about women are not for women only. Women may find these stories more relevant than most men do, but that does not mean that men should not study these parts of the Bible. Men and women may read these stories very differently from each other, but all persons of faith need to hear about these ancient women.

In addition to this conviction, I now have a compulsion. Not long ago, the women of the Old Testament were very unfamiliar to me. Their names rarely appear in sermons and Sunday school lessons, though I think that times are changing and that the situation has improved recently. But there is still so much to do; these stories should not be so rare. Now that I have begun to know these ancient women, they compel me to tell their stories. Their struggles in faith and with faith move me, and I cannot keep myself from telling them. Some stories are just too good—or too tragic—to keep to one's self. I must tell these women's stories, because there is an essential part of faith within them.

Empowered by this conviction and this compulsion, I will tell these stories, but there is still within me a great deal of hesitation. What follows in this book are not these women's stories; they are *my tellings* of their stories. And that's quite a different matter. I would hardly trust anyone else to tell the story of my life and faith; why should others trust me to tell their stories? Certainly my tellings change things from the way that these women would tell their own stories. My experiences are so different from theirs.

I am a young, white male of the late twentieth century, living a comfortable middle-class life as a religious expert in the wealthiest nation in our planet's history. They were women of many different ethnic backgrounds, many ages, and many life situations, but always in the disadvantaged roles assigned to women in their societies. Most of them lived in the poorest, most unsophisticated and politically irrelevant parts of the world. We are thousands of years apart, and it becomes impossible to understand each other completely across all of these gaps.

I think that it is quite likely that others could come closer to capturing the essence of these women's stories. I face too many gulfs of understanding. Today's women do not possess the gender barrier to these texts that I cannot escape. Women of color and women of less privileged social and economic situations share numerous life experiences with these ancient women; I cannot put myself in their place and make those experiences my own. All I can do is listen to the stories, and hear them through the multiple distortions of time and society.

When I listen to these stories, they make me wonder. I wonder what I hear. Do I hear only my own voice, or do I truly hear the voices of these ancient women? Often, I even wonder if these women speak at all. When I read their stories, am I only reading *someone else's* retellings? Women like Eve and Sarah did not put pen to papyrus and produce records of their own stories. Others told the stories for them, and those others were (at least in the vast majority of cases) the wealthy, powerful men who controlled the means of writing. Do we really read their stories, or only the stories that rich elite males want to tell?

This brings us to my fear in writing this book. I fear that I am producing another text about women that merely gives a view from the top, a view that distorts these women's own perspectives. If so, it seems that this text I now write serves only to displace further these women's stories. I have no desire to do that, and yet I know that I will, because that is the (unfortunate) nature of texts—they displace other texts. As hard as I try to displace only the misinterpretations of the biblical texts, I know that I also displace the original texts of these women and the stories that others today would tell. The original texts are long lost, hidden behind the first writing of them, and obscured further by the centuries of retelling, but I am more greatly concerned that another text now could silence the others who would tell their own stories in different ways. So I hope that the readers of this text displace it with their own stories, the text that they write through the actions of life each day, not with the tools of modern academia.

Let me switch metaphors to something I find more helpful.

I have heard the music of these ancient women's lives and faith. They have played this music not with wooden and metal instruments, but with their very lives. In some sense, the music *is* their life. Throughout the ages, the music echoes to where I can hear it. The echoes change some of the tones, but the music is still just as haunting, and I long to play it, too. My own life is a quite different instrument than theirs, so the music sounds very different. I can recognize the tune, but I'm not even sure that others would say that I'm playing the same tune. Others hear it differently, and I imagine that someone will say that I didn't hear it "right." But I have heard what I have heard, and now I will play it as best I can. I love the music, and I want everyone to hear it. If I bumble some of the notes, please understand; I hope that you can still identify the tune.

But my goal is not that you sit and listen to me. I want *you* to play the music, too. The tune is contagious! Pick up your own life and play along. This music will sound quite different when you play it. My hope is that many will play this music, each on a different instrument of life, and that a symphony will result. When there is disagreement and discord, the harmony may stretch close to the breaking point, and the sound may seem unpleasant, but this music has a remarkable ability to withstand our limited ability to play. Some play happier tunes; for others, the song seems mournful. It's all there in the music, really. When we play our parts together, we may begin to understand how the piece should sound.

Chapter 1

Starting the Story

The story starts at the end. That's the paradox of interpretation.

Interpretation always begins at the end of ancient stories, even stories of origins. There's a good reason for that: interpretation requires interpreters, and those interpreters come after the story. When any interpreter begins the study of an ancient story, such as one of the stories from the Bible, one first discovers the many layers of tradition that separate the reader from the text. When we study one of the Old Testament stories, two thousand years or more stand between us and the story. The beginning of interpretation is the interpreter, and we interpreters are *now*, at the end of the the story and at the end of all the history that has happened since the story. Interpretation begins at the end.

In other words, *we* begin to read the text, and when we begin, we must first begin to realize all that has happened since the story. The history *after* the story has made us who we are, and that is where any reading begins—with who we are. Whenever we try to read someone else's story, our own stories come to the front of our minds. Sometimes, our own history can block our reading of the ancient story. We know ourselves, and so we expect this other story to be like our story. This is a dangerous assumption, even though it's an inevitable one.

When the story and the subsequent history form a continuous tradition, the problem may not be so bad. When the text's story is close to our own story, perhaps we can still understand the story. But when our own story is so far away from the ancient story, any

1

reading at all becomes most difficult. The Bible is an ancient book, and that makes it hard to read. Of course, we still affirm that the Bible is valuable and relevant, but its very age can slow us down as we try to read.

The history after these stories of Old Testament women is long; this faith history winds down through the ages until it produces us, and still it keeps going. For today's Christians, the Old Testament is hardly the end of the story. Jesus carries on the story of God's involvement with humanity. In the New Testament, the church's roots receive attention, but the church's development takes another nineteen centuries. We stand at the end of that line. Our history flavors the way we read these texts.

Another problem compounds this when we read the stories about women in the Old Testament. The stories do not conform to the history after the stories. These stories deal with women, but the church's development is most often told as a story of men, leaving far too little room for the kinds of women we find in the Old Testament stories. These ancient women were strong proponents of faith in God. They represent a remarkable variety of ways to live the faith, but as a whole they present us with a shocking truth: there are few stories of women in the last two thousand years with whom we can compare these Old Testament women. These stories are far outside the mainstream of our historical experience, and so our history conflicts with the biblical stories.

Throughout this book, we will strive to hear these ancient stories. At times, this means that we will have to argue with the history and with the ways that the church has historically interpreted these stories. Our goal will be faithfulness to God and to the ancient stories, not necessarily to the history after the stories. But we cannot ignore the history. Not only has it shaped the church, but it has also shaped us, and makes it difficult to read the stories. Before anything else, we must examine in a quick fashion this men's history through which and past which we will read these stories of faith, these ancient stories of Old Testament women.

The History of the Men of Faith

The men's history of faith and the church is a history of the exclusion of women. From the ancient Israelite priesthood and the prophets (who were almost exclusively male) to Jesus' twelve male disciples and the strongly male leadership of the period of the "Church Fathers," we have too often been a faith for men only.[1]

Early Israel's history was certainly a male-oriented one. The heroes of faith in Israel's prehistory were men, such as Abraham and Moses. Though Zipporah and Sarah were prominent figures in those stories (not to mention other women), their names rarely joined the lists of faith's history. God was frequently called "the God of the fathers," and fathers handed down to their sons a special relationship with God. Promises made to one generation reached their fulfillment through the males of the next generation; the blessing stayed in the family, as measured through the male line. Early Israel marginalized women. Women's disadvantage may not have been so great in the realities of that time, but the men who later told the story of those early years emphasized male faithfulness almost to the complete exclusion of women. As time passed, the religious formulations accentuated the male in ever more restricted ways.

When the monarchy arose in Israel, first under Saul's leadership and then with the monarchic dynasty of David and his son Solomon, men grasped ever more firmly the reins of power. When the kings ruled, their power was military to a large degree, and thus the entirely male armies and mercenary forces became the key to attaining and maintaining power. When the kings list their "friends" (a technical term for a political aide) and helpers, the lists are completely male (2 Samuel 8:15–18). The monarchy provided little room for female leadership at all. Queens were generally unimportant in the Israelite monarchy, and the influence of the king's many wives was usually limited to palace intrigue behind the scenes of political power.

Before, during, and after the monarchy, God spoke to the people, both men and women, through priests and prophets. Almost all of them were men, though there were exceptions. Miriam may have carried some of the functions of the priesthood, and some women were prophets, such as Huldah (2 Kings 22:14),

---

[1]The notion of an unbroken line of faith throughout all time is a relatively recent one; the ancients were much more concerned with their experiences with God than about a progression through the texts. The idea of a "salvation history" is even more recent, and many biblical scholars now believe this idea to be misleading, in no small part because it negates the value of underrepresented texts, such as those about women.

but these were the exception. The priesthood was usually restricted to membership in particular families, and only men could become priests. Thus, the people's most frequent image of human connection to God was entirely male. This combined with the masculine language and predominantly male images for the deity to create a sense in which God was perceived as male. Though ancient Israel knew the problems with idolatry, they still created for themselves an image of God as a male, often using the same language for God as they used for human male leaders. Though prophecy was much less institutional than the priesthood, this general understanding of God's maleness certainly influenced the people, forming the notion that God could only communicate through those people most like God, males.

Later in Israel's history, after the monarchy, leadership often appeared in the form of assemblies, marking a mild degree of democratization after the complete restriction of power to a small group of elites during the monarchy. However, these assemblies consisted only of males. Usually, these were the oldest, wealthiest, most powerful men of the community. Each was a head of a house, which may well indicate a man who rules over his own family and other closely related families (Ezra 10:16–17). Throughout the years, this assembly grew both in formality and in power. By Jesus' time, the Sanhedrin was a council with official responsibilities and power over the whole people. Again, its membership was exclusively male. Though these assemblies increase the number of people who share the community's power, this system still concentrates all power in the hands of the men. Women are utterly disenfranchised.[2]

The traditions about Jesus offer a breath of fresh air in this stultifying repression of women. Jesus talked with women in the same tones with which he talked with men and told parables that included women as the heroes of faith. Women joined the groups that supported Jesus, offering even financial support in an era when society sharply limited women's ability to own property. His large traveling company included several women who were prominent in the Gospel traditions, such as Mary (James' and Joseph's mother), Mary Magdalene, Zebedee's wife, Salome,

---

[2]Of course, every society has possessed many other tools for disenfranchisement, which have both reinforced the disadvantage of some women and enabled other women to gain certain types of power, often separating them from their sisters.

Joanna, the sisters Mary and Martha, and Jesus' own mother, Mary. Jesus' inclusion of women coincided with his consistent embracing of disadvantaged persons, such as the poor, foreigners (especially the hated Gentiles and Samaritans), children, and lepers. Jesus treated all humans equally and fairly, offering all of them their rightful place among the people of God. This would greatly increase the options available to women in that society. Jesus was remarkable in his valuation of women, especially when compared to the misogynist tendencies of Jesus' inherited religious traditions.

Though Jesus provided a new and enhanced role for women, the church's retellings of those stories play down the presence of women. Within the Gospels themselves, this pattern already begins, but it reaches its full force within later church tradition. When we focus on Jesus' followers, we think immediately of the twelve disciples as models for leadership and as examples of true intimacy with Jesus. Of course, such a focus ignores the Gospels' own insistence that the disciples did not understand Jesus nearly as well as others did, such as several of Jesus' women followers. Still, the twelve disciples have become for us the model of closeness with Jesus. The more that we accept and propagate such an emphasis, the less room we allow for the affirmation of women's roles in Jesus' own ministry.

Within the next phase of the early church's existence, the process of reexcluding women continues and intensifies. Our tradition did not preserve the writings of any of the early women leaders of the church, despite Paul's repeated mention of women who were active in all forms of leadership and faith. The roles of women quickly disappear into the background, where they had been before Jesus' ministry. By the end of the New Testament period, the writings insist that women take the same places within life that the society at large assigned to them. The early church soon forgot the myriad ways that the transformative power of Jesus' teachings and actions had changed life for women by including them in every phase of faith and church life.

Within the next generations of the church, the situation simply got worse. With the centralizing of authority in bishops and nonlocal leaders, more power resided in male hands once more. For several decades after Jesus, women had shared authority and responsibility on the local level, but the church never accepted women into the larger roles as the church invented new patterns of leadership that enhanced power for a few and wrenched it away from women. This period of church history is often referred to as the time of the Church Fathers, offering a clear description of the impossibility of roles for women. In later centuries, the church once more allowed contributions by a wider variety of people, but the traditions of male authority were already well entrenched. When monks and theologians began their writings and teachings that still influence theology today, almost all of these authorities were male. Though there were many influential women in medieval times, we have preserved fewer of their contributions.

In modern times, women have resumed leadership roles only recently and still in limited numbers. Many denominations still deny ordination to women, and very few women have risen in the denominational hierarchies. Women pastors and professors of religion are still rare, though their numbers are growing steadily. In some branches of the Christian faith, women and men may share equally in the business of the faith within a few decades.

Of course, there is much more to the experience of faith than the business of the church and positions in the hierarchies. We must not ignore these hierarchical concerns, because they affect much of the life of faith and communicate to women of faith a certain secondary status that often works against women's intimacy with God. But faith exists independently of the church's bureaucracies and systems of power and control. Women have much more access to faith than to the hierarchies. Women retain much influence at local levels of leadership, though often in unofficial roles, and women often possess a deeper, more mature faith than many men.[3] Women's capacity to find support within communities of faith, to share their faith with the next generation, and to allow their faith to shape their lives is unquestioned. Though the male hierarchies limit these capacities, women continue to live their faith in remarkable and powerfully effective ways.

The history of the church is a history of men in positions of power and leadership. But the reality of many congregations today is the vigor of women's faith. The history, especially the favored retellings of that history, and the reality of faith experience conflict with each other sharply. As in most human endeavors, those in power usually manage to win the conflict and to

---

[3]For examples, see any of the recent publications or video presentations by the Search Institute.

attempt control of others. Thus, the male history of the church serves as a way to limit women's faith by directing it into narrowly prescribed areas. This men's history not only avoids responsiveness to the needs of women's faith, but it can actively attack their faith in a struggle to attain and retain mastery.

Stories of Women's Faith

The male history of the church is antagonistic to women's faith in the many forms in which women experience it. This strong line of history throughout the church's existence serves only to dominate the way that both men and women can experience and express their faith. This male retelling of history is, of course, a distortion of what really happened; all historical retellings distort the realities. In the same way, no two people seeing the same event at the same time describe it in identical words. Each observer tells the story in different ways, and each way of telling and retelling shifts the details, distorting the event. Histories distort reality, and a one-sided history such as that told by the church's powerful works against the authentic experiences of faith that are possible through intimacy with God. History strives to limit the form of faith into predictable, acceptable forms, and our history tells us that those normative forms belong to men, but not to women.

In the midst of this history, do we even know how to hear women's stories?[4] The thundering drone of this one dominant historical retelling threatens to drown out all other voices, especially the voices of women and others who are underrepresented. New voices threaten the dominance and the singularity of the one history. Other stories, such as women's stories, threaten to disrupt the solidarity of history. So how do we hear those stories over the noise of the history? How do we tell those stories with fresh voices?

First, we must recognize that these women's stories, both ancient and modern, will be stories from the periphery of the church. Men have so long controlled the central, powerful posi-

---

[4]See Carol A. Newsom and Sharon H. Ringe, eds., *The Women's Bible Commentary* (Louisville: Westminster/John Knox Press, 1992), for a wonderful work that discusses the women of each biblical book. This volume provides a major contribution to hearing biblical women and understanding the fullness of the biblical story.

tions that women's voices can come only from the edges. They will represent roles and ideas that do not represent the preponderant retellings of history and the dominant institutions of the church. Women's stories are not the same as leaders' histories for at least one reason: women have not been leaders, because of how the leadership has restricted itself to men.

One article of faith can strengthen our attempts to hear women's stories. We have confidence that God works through all persons who share an intimacy of faith with God. The church has allowed men to express this work of God through formal leadership positions and has typically disallowed women from such offices. But the church's harping insistence on the centrality of masculinity can never stop God's willingness to work through all people, both women and men. The task, then, is ours: we must learn how to recognize God's working through women. This is necessary for us if we are to know and experience fully God's work within the world. God works through women and men and we must see both.

The Old Testament offers us remarkable resources for understanding how God works through women. These stories of ancient women of faith represent a wide variety of ways in which God works. This variety provides us with a survey of the marvelous range of possible expressions for women's faith. Examining these stories can teach us how to include all persons within our own religious practices and beliefs today.

Many of the stories about Old Testament women are extremely painful because they show the horrible ways in which men of faith have treated women of faith. These stories can prove helpful for us if we remember to speak forth their pain clearly, and to recognize the pain within today's women of faith. Other of the Old Testament stories are more hopeful, showing us the ways things can be. From these we can gain a sense of our goals. Other stories show us methods to reach those goals, offering concrete suggestions about including all of God's people in all aspects of faith.

These different emphases within these stories provide us with a much-needed spectrum of women's stories. If we truly will create a church that includes all of God's people, then we must recognize the problems of women and face these problems squarely, unblinkingly, yet not insensitively. We must feel the pain of ancient women and modern women before we can truly begin to address that pain in relevant ways. But pain and despair are not enough to bring about the changes. We must also have a vision of the life that God intends, in which women and men share their lives and their faith together. We also need plans for the change, or else the whole discussion stops short of the possibilities for action.

This book presents several of the stories of Old Testament women in roughly chronological order. First, we will examine the ways of life for women in earliest Israel. What did it mean for them to worship their God, whose name was Yahweh? How did they experience God and live their faith? How did men and women live their faith together and apart? Within this context, we can read the story of the first woman, Eve, with new eyes. We can listen more attentively to Eve's story and hear the concerns of the women who would tell that story as their own. These questions provide us with a glimpse into very early times, giving us opportunity to see the changes that come about in the years of the monarchy, when the society imposes increasing limits on women's roles and on the possibilities for women to express their faith in God.

Other women, in addition to Eve, were the subjects of early stories about women of faith, but for many of them, silence marks the tellings of their stories. Discerning women such as Sarah is almost impossible, because the history of Abraham and other men suppresses the stories of others around them, including the women whose lives intertwine with theirs. Women's silence reaches its chilling apex on a mountainside when Lot's nameless wife receives a permanent silencing. Never again will she speak, and in these haunting stories, the men seem to prefer that women stay silent, even about their faith. When women stay silent, the men often treat them as objects, and many of these stories in books such as Genesis and Judges present women as objects for the men to buy and sell. Procreation is women's chief function; the resultant children can also be bought and sold by the controlling men; and one almost senses that labor and birth should be cloaked with the same silence that stifles almost all telling of women's stories.

Elsewhere in Genesis, we find stories of women who take charge. They refuse the silence that men would push upon them and give voice to their own lives. Likewise, the Old Testament provides stories of several women who proclaim their faith in clear, unmistakable terms. Ancient women could speak their faith only at great risk; the male establishment rarely accepted such statements as true expressions of divine intimacy. But some of the women spoke anyway, risking the great cost of the powerful men's wrath. Through these stories and others in the book of Judges, we can view startling images of women's power to speak and women's powerlessness in the face of the expected silence.

After the early years described in the book of Genesis and the days of settling in the Promised Land as told in the book of Judges came the monarchy. The advent of kingship in Israel changed the structures of leadership and greatly restricted the opportunities for women to express faith. Increasingly, men considered women as property and treated them as such. Some women could attain some limited influence in the society, but this happened only rarely. The prophets offer clear examples of these tendencies. Though at least one woman was a prophet, this role fell almost exclusively to men, and they discussed women in strong, striking terms that often degraded women. Abusive relationships in which women suffered physically, emotionally, and sexually became suitable metaphors for God's treatment of the people. Yet surely God does not condone abuse in any form.

The monarchy produced educational systems that trained scribes in business, bureaucracy, and other matters, and they revered wisdom as the highest virtue. At times, these scribes and sages talked about wisdom as a human woman. Lady Wisdom was God's partner in creation, and human participation in wisdom was a means to partnership with God. This provides one of the most positive female images in the entire Old Testament, and truly in the whole Bible. Another related positive portrayal of women is in the Song of Songs, which is rather explicit sexual material that affirms the sexuality of both women and men as joyful elements of God's creation.

After the monarchy, several short stories about women present a number of views of what women should be. The story of Ruth tells of two women, Ruth and Naomi, and the mutually supportive relationship that they form in the midst of affliction and hardship. Together, they learn to live with men but without the constrictive dependence upon men that their society fostered. The book of Esther depicts a strong woman who knows what she must do in order to save her people and who performs that task with skill and efficiency, bringing salvation to all the Jews. In the apocryphal books that are recognized as canonical scripture by some Christian traditions but not by most Protestants, several more stories display other dimensions of women. In the book of Tobit, Sarah's prayer and piety bring her a blessed life and strong family relationships. Judith, in the book that bears her name, lectures the town's elders on what is truly pious and proper. Susanna's story is one of purity protected against the wiles of men. Together, these stories form a remarkable mosaic of possibilities for women's lives and women's faith.

After the End

Our own reading of these ancient stories starts at the end. We read them after the stories end and after the history that separated us from these stories. When the reading starts, history ends and our experiencing of these texts opens up fresh new possibilities. Within us as interpreters, these ancient stories can create a new history. The beginning of reading is the end of history, and after history ends comes the present in which we read. Within this present, all possibilities surround us. Though the history limits us, these stories break down those limits and explode the boundaries that others would place on our faith and its expression as women and men in this new world. These new possibilities are radically new, and a fresh faith is the reward for those who accept this challenge. The new possibilities awaiting within these stories are frightening, because they are so wide open and new. Though they can scare us, they can also empower us to create a new history in which God's people join together in the service of our one God. This possibility is exciting, for it reaches ever closer to the fulfillment of God's own desires for our lives. Still, it frightens, because it means life outside the limits of our history's restriction. It means constructing new stories for ourselves that express God's intimacy with us in fresh ways.

After history ends, the present arrives, but there is also a future that awaits. The future of our faith is ours and God's to create. We build this future ourselves as we hear these ancient stories of faith and allow this faith to energize us. This new future can build upon the history, if we are careful to select its strengths and avoid its problems and weaknesses. Also, we can build our future on the stories that we read, stories that often defy the history that has come down to us. No matter where we build, we must firmly fix our attention on what can be, because our goal should be nothing short of the potential for which God creates and re-creates us. That potential includes many characteristics, but we must affirm one of them continually as we read and interpret these ancient stories of women's faith: our faith and practice and church of today must include women fully if we are to reach the potential that God desires for our faith. God's goal is a lofty one—the inclusion of all people in the people of God, who live their lives in faith and who give their lives in effective, empowered service to our one loving, striving God.

Chapter 2

Women in Early Israel

What was life like for women in ancient Israel, in the times of the Old Testament? This question is a complicated one, fraught with several difficult problems, but we need an answer before we can begin to discuss the stories about these women and their lives. We must know how they lived in order to understand the stories that they tell.

The first problem is that the Old Testament tells about a thousand years' worth of history. From the earliest days to the end of the biblical material, things changed. Women's situations were not at all static over this millennium. Thus, when we talk about women's daily lives in "biblical times," we must be more specific about the time frame.

A second problem is the issue of sources. The Bible does not answer all the questions that we could possibly ask. In fact, the Old Testament rarely discusses daily life. Instead, the stories tell of special occasions, which may or may not be representative of a regular day. Furthermore, the biblical sources tell us their stories each from one perspective, usually from the vantage point of the rich and powerful men who controlled the society and the religion. We have many stories about kings in the Old Testament, but rather few stories about common folk. That information is much harder to derive from the biblical texts. Instead, we have to read around the bias of the elite authors, who may themselves have lived a century or more after the events that they describe.

These two problems, the large scale of Old Testament history and the distance and bias of the sources, combine to make the description of earliest Israel most difficult. Many scholars now agree that we cannot offer an adequate depiction of life or history in the periods described in the books of Genesis through Deuteronomy. Those books now appear to us in a form that dates from later in Israel's history. Though these first five books (also called the Pentateuch) offer important information about these early times, they also reflect the monarchic and postmonarchic times in which they were written as reminiscences and retellings of former periods in their history, and it becomes very difficult to tell the difference.

However, we can construct portrayals of Israel in the two centuries before the rise of the monarchy. This period is often called Early Israel, and contains the time periods discussed by the books of Joshua and Judges. During these two hundred years, the people formed a common character, united by a similar way of life. They began as small scattered groups of people and ended this transitional time with the beginnings of the monarchy and the additional structure that implies. Thus, during this time Israel became settled in its life in the land, creating a way of life that was somewhat distinctive and that formed the foundation for their later development. Our attempts at describing this period find a strong ally in archaeology, because there are substantive discoveries of relevant material in Israel for this time. Together, the biblical and archaeological sources show us some of what life was like in the period 1200–1000 B.C.E., if we look carefully.[1]

The Old Days

This transition period began with Israel as a very diverse group. The usual understanding recounts this as a time of military conquest. God told the people to enter into the land of Canaan and to defeat it with force, killing all of the people inside the region and taking the Canaanites' land for themselves (Joshua

---

[1]The terms B.C.E. and C.E. are used for dates, standing for Before the Common Era and Common Era, respectively. These measures of dates are used by Jewish and Christian scholars who interpret the Bible in an interfaith context, and they refer to the same years as the more familiar measures B.C. (Before Christ) and A.D. (*Anno Domini*, or Year of the Lord).

1:1–6). But the Old Testament's stories were somewhat different. The Israelites never conquered the Canaanites. After a few battles, the Israelites stopped the fighting, and lived among the Canaanites in peace. Many of the inhabitants of the land joined the Israelites in common ventures, and there may even have been substantial intermarriage in addition to the economic ties forged in those years. The Israelites maintained their own towns, their own communities, their own culture, and their own religion—but they did not drive the Canaanites out of the land.

The Israelites and the Canaanites did not intermingle with each other in ways that destroyed the differences between their independent cultures. Assimilation was not the chief mode of coexistence. Instead, they lived next to each other with complete awareness of the other and with communication between them, but without an antagonistic attitude that assumed their cultures were mutually exclusive and also without indiscriminate mixing of their cultures and faiths. A simple distinction promoted this separation by which the Israelites lived among the Canaanites without being Canaanite themselves. The Canaanites were urban and the Israelites were rural. Though the Old Testament never explicitly claims this distinction, the evidence is plain. Canaanites are always part of a city, such as Jericho, Ai, or Jebus. The same texts refer to the Israelites by tribes; they inhabited regions, not cities. The Israelites would live in small villages in the hilly countryside, leaving the cities for the Canaanites. Though there would be trade and communication between the two peoples who shared the same territory, the lines between them were quite distinct, and they could maintain separate cultures as urban and rural people have done in many civilizations since.[2]

Canaanite cities contained more than just the high rises on top of hills, surrounded by strong walls. These cities (or perhaps *city-states* would be the better term) also controlled a certain amount of farm land around the city walls, including small villages within that valley region. These farms and villages provided the food for the Canaanite cities; in return, the cities provided the villages with trade privileges and protection from marauders and

---

[2]For discussions of early Israel's sociological conditions, see Robert B. Coote, *Early Israel: A New Horizon* (Minneapolis: Fortress Press, 1990); and Norman K. Gottwald, *The Tribes of Yahweh: A Sociology of the Religion of Liberated Israel, 1250-1050 B.C.E.* (Maryknoll, New York: Orbis Books, 1979).

from the attacks of nearby city-states. The cities controlled rural life and operated the rural villages (often called "daughter-cities") to the profit of the local city's king, the royal family, and the aristocrats. The elite experienced great privilege from this system, which guaranteed the workers' exploitation in order to supply the benefits for the rich few. But the farmers had one advantage: the farmland in the valleys around the fortified hilltop cities was some of the most productive land in the whole region. Even if the taxes were extremely high, at least they had easy land to farm. Canaanite life was stable and protected, lived according to a system that had functioned for centuries.

The Israelites lived a very different life. By choosing to live apart from the Canaanite cities, they lost the benefits of that old, traditional system. Perhaps the biggest change was that the Israelites had no access to the best farmland. Instead, they had to live and farm in the hill country, where the ground was much less capable of supporting them. They had to work much harder to get enough food for themselves. Also, they lost the military protection and the trading privileges of the Canaanite cities, so that they could not count on anyone but themselves to help them through their hard times. Though the Israelites lost the benefits of the Canaanites' secure, stable existence, they also escaped the disadvantages of life under Canaanite control. They became free, giving substance to the dream of political freedom and self-determination fostered by Moses in Egypt. The Israelites controlled their own lives and could worship in any way that they wanted, and so their worship of Yahweh grew from a small dissent group within Egypt to a whole new way of belief and life. They believed that God had called them into being and created them as a people in order to live this kind of free life.

Though the Israelites were free, their life was certainly not easy. Farming was nearly impossible. They kept needing more and more laborers just to farm enough food to survive. They had no protection against the dangers and inevitabilities of life, such as a raid, famine, plague, pestilence, destructive weather, accidental death, or other such calamities. Since they were living on a thin margin of subsistence, any of these disasters could destroy the delicate balance of their existence and trigger a crisis. Over time, these sorts of disasters were sure to happen many times. But when problems multiplied, a true emergency occurred, and the Israelites searched for radical new solutions for this life-and-death crisis.

Crisis and Solution

In the hill country outside and around the Canaanite city-states of Palestine, the Israelites lived a tenuous existence. With some technological innovations, they were able to eke out a living from the hills. They learned to terrace the slopes so that they could increase the amount of land suitable for growing crops. They also developed some techniques for storing rain-water in cisterns so that they could distribute the water onto the terraces. Otherwise, the water would run off down the hill and they would lose the moisture so desperately needed for survival in a climate that was mostly arid.

The innovations of cisterns and terraces enabled survival from their meager farms in the hills, but these were not easy solutions. Terracing required the moving of large amounts of soil in order to create level strips of farmland along the hillsides. This was a very labor-intensive farming process. Likewise, irrigation by cistern involved digging the pits, lining them with special material to prevent excess seepage, and then carrying the water from the cisterns to the fields. These technological advances merely allowed subsistence; they did not produce increases in the crops grown from this barely sufficient soil. Thus, the produc-tion of crops in the hills would require more labor than farming in the Canaanite-controlled valleys, even before one considers the additional labor investment of the terraces and cisterns.

This was the primary factor in the creation of crisis. Israelite farming required high amounts of labor for mere subsistence. When the Canaanites forced the Israelites further into the hills, the Israelites lost even more arable land. Labor needs rose to emergency levels. In response to this crisis, early Israel did everything in its power to increase its labor and thus its produc-tivity. What resulted was one of the world's most amazing feats of social engineering. Though it succeeded admirably, the side effects are still present in much of the world.

In short, the Israelites increased their labor by increasing their population, and that meant increasing their rate of childbirth. Through a series of laws, customs, and values, the Israelites restructured their society to emphasize and maximize childbirth. This had important effects on women's lives.[3]

---

[3]For a much more detailed presentation of this thesis, see Carol Meyers, *Discovering Eve: Ancient Israelite Women in Context* (Oxford: Oxford University Press, 1988).

Women's Lives

Before the crisis, early Israelite life was rather egalitarian. Of course, equality meant a very different thing to these ancient people than it does to us. We talk of equality in terms of equal pay for equal work, or equal opportunity to advance in careers, or freedom of choice of lifestyle for all people. For the early Israelites, equality in life meant that both women and men worked in the fields each day for their survival. In their subsistence economy, they were poor rural folk who each had no choice but to work hard just to get enough food to eat. Everyone worked out in the field, and both men and women did mostly the same types of work. Back-breaking farm labor was the way of life for everyone, including women, men, and children, too.

Though this system had worked in the past, the changing situation necessitated a new strategy for survival. Because more workers were needed in order for people to survive, early Israel valued childbearing. This valuation was not done lightly. Israel's emphasis on childbearing was a serious reorientation of their life priorities, and it was not without cost and risk. In the ancient world, childbirth was a dangerous, life-threatening event. In fact, childbirth was the leading cause of death among women. Certainly, the earlier society had not forbidden children or discouraged large families, but they realized that pregnancy was a dangerous thing, not to be undertaken lightly. The previous strategy required each person's labor each day, and childbearing would provide one possible future worker in exchange for risking the life of a woman who was an important contributor to the family's present survival. Only when the need for quick population growth reached higher levels did it become sensible to do everything possible to encourage that growth, no matter what the cost.

This reorientation of strategy created new laws and customs. In the new system, pregnant women received a greater level of protection. They lost their equal functions in order to increase the likelihood that the child would survive. Sexual activity was restricted in ways thought to maximize birth rates. Women's sexuality became subject to community control. There arose a marriage type called polygyny, in which one man could have multiple wives. The reason for this was clear: it would maximize the number of births.[4] This pattern is familiar in the earlier Old

---

[4]This may reflect a situation in which there were more women than men, perhaps because of male deaths in warfare or some other cause. If

Testament stories; one thinks of Jacob's two wives and two concubines whose combined production was twelve sons and at least one daughter. With this type of marriage pattern and an emphasis on childbearing, a quick population increase would be quite possible.[5]

This reorientation of society also moved women out of the more strenuous forms of farm work. This diminished the incidence of miscarriage, increasing the birth rate. However, this shift also changed women's roles. No longer were women equal partners with men in the fields; women now received the special protection of the law. The community recognized that their survival depended upon a contribution that only women could make, and so the customs and laws evolved to emphasize this contribution of population growth while decreasing the emphasis on women's agricultural contributions to a corresponding degree. Women's productivity did not decline; it remained constant or increased while the *types* of productivity expected and encouraged shifted.

In response to crisis, the society encouraged childbirth and correspondingly decreased the emphasis on women's involvement in tasks that men could do just as well. This worked toward a solution of the crisis by increasing the population, providing over the span of years the larger labor force that would enable life and livelihood as a hill country community.[6] Of course, this massive shift of societal resources was not a conscious decision; it was a natural response to the situations that the community faced in its daily living. However, the changes occurred in response to a crisis, and these changes were highly effective,

---

women did outnumber men, then monogamy (marriage between one man and one woman) would have resulted in women without male sexual partners, decreasing the number of births. Also, a shortage of men would explain the emphasis on the production of sons, rather than children in general. Of course, there are many other possible reasons.

[5]Marriage was also strictly controlled; mates were selected by families who knew each other. Venereal diseases may have been a factor; these diseases spread more quickly by contact with outside groups and can sharply limit live-birth rates. See Carol L. Meyers, "The Roots of Restriction: Women in Early Israel," in *The Bible and Liberation: Political and Social Hermeneutics,* ed. Norman K. Gottwald (Maryknoll, New York: Orbis Books, 1983), pp. 289–306.

[6]The time span would be about a decade, since child labor was the norm.

resolving the crisis within a decade or two. After the population increased sufficiently, then these nonegalitarian laws and norms were no longer needed since the society had already attained a more optimum population.

The society protected women and required less in other duties because of the need for reproduction, but quite possibly these laws were meant to be temporary, lasting only until the population was increased. But once the population and labor force grew, the laws remained the same. Crisis forced a temporary inequality, but the inequality resulted in power structures that did not give up their advantages after the fact. Crisis bred temporary, purposeful inequality; temporary inequality bred permanent, structural inequality, and over the years, this inequality only grew worse.

For these ancient people, economic rationales (such as the one just presented) would never have sufficed to explain social events. Instead, the people would also perceive their lives in terms of their faith and their religion. Though a move to increase childbearing would be natural in the face of such a crisis, these ancient people of faith would have understood this new emphasis as God's will. Not only did they perceive this strong emphasis on childbirth as God's will for the solution of crisis, but they understood it as God's permanent will for the people. Thus a temporary solution became embedded within the structure of the religion, and thus it became permanent, since religions tend to preserve and conserve their past. If this crisis produced a *religious* emphasis on childbirth, then we must next investigate the religion of early Israel.

Yahweh and the Gods of Other Peoples

The usual summary of Israel's history emphasizes that the Israelites developed a monotheistic religion. That is, the Israelites believed that there was only one God, whose name was Yahweh. Some scholars have suggested that a better term for early Israel's religion was *monolatry*, which is the worship and service of only one God. There might be other gods in the world, but Israel would only obey Yahweh, not any of the other deities. However, both of these notions oversimplify early Israel's complex religious milieu.

In its early years, Israel lived in the middle of Canaan. The numerous small tribes of Israel crouched on the hills between the lush Canaanite towns. The two groups probably shared some sort of trade and communication. This meant that they were quite aware of each other's religion. The Canaanite religion centered on two gods, El and Baal, and two goddesses, Asherah and Anat. El and Baal are both terms that the Old Testament at times uses to describe Israel's God, Yahweh. *El* means God, and *Baal* means Lord. These are not so much names for God as titles, in something of the same way that we use the terms *God* and *Lord* today. El and Asherah were the elder gods, and Baal and Anat were the younger deities. Though Canaanites also believed in the existence of several other deities, they did not worship these others. El, Asherah, Baal, and Anat formed the core of the Canaanite religion.[7] Of these gods, El was most like Yahweh, though Yahweh also shared some characteristics with Baal.

Israel's emphasis on the worship of only one God was not complete. From Aaron's fashioning of a golden bull to the kings' construction of shrines for other gods, Israel was involved with the worship of other gods. For those who lived in a time when most people believed in many gods, the restriction of worship to only one God was problematic. The emphasis on a sole God shaped Israelite religion in directions that were previously unexplored. Canaanite gods were each responsible for limited parts of life, but Israel's Yahweh was responsible for everything that gods could do. Yahweh had to be responsible for more because there were no other gods with whom Yahweh could share the work. This created a tendency for the Israelites to ascribe to Yahweh the attributes of other deities; they claimed Yahweh could do anything and everything that any of the Canaanite gods could do.

The opposite tendency also occurred. Faced with actions that Yahweh was not doing, some of the Israelites would worship other deities. Though this was not the approved religion by Israel's leaders, many of the people found a need for more help than Yahweh seemed to provide. When they had specific problems, they would seek out a deity who was thought to "specialize" in those matters. For this reason, Baal became a popular deity with some Israelites, because Baal was a storm god who specialized in bringing rain for the crops. When prayers to Yahweh

---

[7]Reconstructing Canaanite religion is a speculative matter because of the relative lack of information. The presentation here simplifies matters too much in the interest of clarity. For more information, see technical works such as Mark S. Smith, *The Early History of God: Yahweh and the Other Deities in Ancient Israel* (San Francisco: Harper and Row, 1990).

did not result in adequate rain, it made a certain sense to some Israelites to pray to Baal, in case that would work. This religion was pragmatic; the people sought any divine help that they could get from any deity who would listen and respond.

Of course, for Israelites the worship of other deities was not as well defined as it was for other peoples such as the Canaanites. The Israelites were accustomed to perceiving Yahweh with a wide variety of attributes. The Canaanites recognized two chief deities who were unmistakably male and two who were obviously female. Each of the gods had separate and clearly defined tasks, but Yahweh did everything. Thus, it made sense to think of Yahweh in different images at different times. We today make the theological assertion that God is bigger than our words. No matter how we describe God, there is always more to God than what we have just said. No human image or idea completely exhausts the multifaceted being of God. In the same way, these ancient people of faith worshiped Yahweh at different times with different words, images, and titles, reflecting the people's changing needs.[8] Perhaps the Israelites, when using a prayer originally written to another deity, thought that they were simply addressing another attribute of Yahweh.

Regardless of the exact understanding of Yahweh's relationship to other gods of other peoples, the Israelites were certainly aware of the wide theological variety found among their neighbors. As their own worship focused more particularly on Yahweh as the only God, two complementary tendencies would appear: the Israelites would ascribe more and more different notions to Yahweh, and they would at times worship other gods when Yahweh seemed to be ineffective in meeting a specific need. This overall religious situation took on special dimensions among the Israelite women.

Women's Faith in Early Israel

At its root, religion is an attempt to shape and control faith. In the Israelite worship of Yahweh, the religious leaders who exer-

---

[8]This also reflects the current modern situation with numerous Christian denominations, all of which claim to worship the same God but use different words and ideas to describe that God. There is no reason to think that any one expression is necessarily wrong just because it disagrees with another formulation. Instead, the full range of expressions may actually come closer to the reality of God than any one denomination's terminology and theology.

cised that control were male, and their gender influenced the ways in which the religion developed. In particular, they were quick to attribute to Yahweh those things that they desired. This meant that Yahweh was seen early in Israel's history as warrior and as God of rain. These were primarily men's concerns, though war and crops certainly affected the whole community, and thus Yahweh became a God with special appeal to the Israelite men.

Of course, the Israelites' descriptions of God did not change God's nature. Yahweh did not "become" a rain god just because the religious leaders proclaimed God as such. These Israelites could not control God at all. However, the religious leaders could control how the people thought about God. Increasingly, the religious leaders encouraged the Israelites to think about God as a man's god, with war, crops, and also national identity as chief concerns. Women's concerns remained unaddressed by the religion. But the religion could not limit Yahweh, and the biblical witness is consistent that Yahweh's concerns always reach wider than our religion comprehends.

What did the Israelite women want from their religion? What was the nature of these women's faith? At this great distance of time and culture, it is exceedingly difficult to answer these questions. If the male religious leaders ignored the concerns of women, then what did the women do to meet their faith needs? Three options present themselves immediately. First, women could worship Yahweh as defined by the male leaders, ignoring their own spiritual needs and worshiping a god of war and crops. Second, they could define Yahweh differently within themselves, concentrating on other images for Yahweh as caring and providing. Third, they could worship other deities, focusing on those that other religious leaders defined in ways that were sensitive to women's lives.

Probably, at least some women chose each one of these options at different points in Israel's history. Certainly we see the performance of the first option, traditional worship of Yahweh, occurring in the lives of many Old Testament women. The second option, worshiping Yahweh by different descriptions, may be reflected in the feminine imagery for Yahweh that is present in many locations in the Old Testament. However, this meant a direct challenge to the authority of the male religious leaders, disputing the rights of humans to describe Yahweh. Many women also chose the third option and worshiped other deities, especially goddesses, in response to their own life situations.

Goddess worship in ancient Israel is attested by both biblical and archaeological data. Some of this goddess worship was very much like orthodox biblical religion, but the religious leaders insisted on the worship of only one god. It may well be that some women did worship Yahweh with these attributes, since the concepts were not antithetical to the traditional religion. Instead, there was a difference of emphasis. Goddess worship was more likely to focus on safety rather than conquest, on health rather than wealth, and on surviving childbirth rather than producing children.

A large number of the rural people throughout Israel's history, both women and men, worshiped Yahweh and a goddess, such as Asherah. In fact, the worship of Yahweh and Asherah also occurred within the central Jerusalem temple itself later in Israel's history. Possibly, the people saw this as worshiping a divine couple, the King and Queen of Heaven, with the names Yahweh and Asherah.[9]

The prophet Jeremiah comments on the worship of the Queen of Heaven. Jeremiah 7:18 offers a brief remark about this worship: "the children gather wood; the fathers kindle the fire; the women knead dough; all work to make cakes for the Queen of Heaven." The worship is a corporate, family experience, involving children and fathers as well as the women. This is not a "women's religion" that leaves out men; it is an inclusive practice. In Jeremiah 44:15–25, the people complain to the prophet that he must be wrong in his insistence on the worship of Yahweh alone. After all, they argue, when they worshiped the Queen of Heaven as well, they prospered and had food. The pragmatism of religion enters again. The people desire the worship of whichever deity would provide them with life and livelihood.[10]

Jeremiah and the other religious leaders press for the official position of worshiping Yahweh alone. Throughout Israel's history, monotheism became increasingly entrenched within the religion.

---

[9]Two parallels are obvious. First, the modern Mormon belief of God and God's (nameless) wife is not far from this suggestion. Second, orthodox Christian belief in one God with three parts (described as Father, Son, and Holy Spirit, or some other formulation) is a similar solution to the problem of a monotheistic God with multiple attributes and concerns.

[10]For more on these Jeremiah texts, see Susan Ackerman, "'And the Women Knead Dough': The Worship of the Queen of Heaven in Sixth-Century Judah," in *Gender and Difference in Ancient Israel,* ed. Peggy L. Day (Minneapolis: Fortress Press, 1989), pp. 109–124.

These religious leaders desired that all Israelites worship only Yahweh, seeking everything they need from Yahweh and from the official religion. This insistence placed extreme pressures on the forms of religion that were more tailored to women's faith. The leaders expected women to join without question to the religion that the men had shaped. Some of the women rebelled and sought other deities; others gave up on their own needs and stayed within the accepted, official religion.

Perhaps the better solution is to realize Yahweh's multifaceted nature and desire to meet all faith needs of all people. Had the religious leaders of the ancient Israelites allowed the worship of Yahweh to contain more elements that were responsive to women's needs, perhaps there would not have been the tendencies to look elsewhere to meet those faith needs. Though it was highly problematic for anyone to reject the worship of Yahweh in order to seek other gods, these women were not rejecting Yahweh. They may have added to the official worship, and they may have rejected the leaders' notions of Yahweh's limits, but they did not reject Yahweh. The roots of the problem rested within the unwillingness of religious leaders to allow Yahweh to respond to women's needs. Yahweh certainly desires to be the God of all the people, both men and women; when religious leaders of any time describe accurately this desire of God, then we can enjoy a religion that responds to faith and does not limit true faith in God.

Chapter 3

First Woman

The study of women of faith in the Old Testament faces numerous problems; the first two chapters have dealt with several of them. Another difficulty is that many of the stories themselves are thoroughly unfamiliar. Few people in today's churches know the stories of, for instance, Jephthah's daughter, or Gomer. But the story of Eve faces no such predicament. The story of Genesis 2—3 is one of the most widely known stories of the whole Bible. God creates two humans, first Adam and then Eve, in a wonderfully lush paradise of a garden called Eden. There enters an evil snake that tempts the woman Eve, and then Eve teaches Adam sin. In anger, God throws both of them out of paradise, and sentences them to lives of punishment and pain out in the world. In passing, we also learn that God has created humans for camaraderie and that the task of humans is to multiply and subdue the earth. At least, this is the story as traditionally told.

The story is familiar; we tell it often. We have already taken the first step toward interpretation—we know the text. But where do we go next? Knowing the story can be a help, since it saves some of the early work of keeping the characters straight in our minds. It also motivates us to figure out the story, since we already have an investment in the text itself. But our prior knowledge presents us with problems, too. This preconceived interpretation of the text can cast a spell on us, blinding us to the possibilities that we have never seen before. The story has become part of our received history, and that history demonstrates to us the priorities of the male religious leaders who teach it to us. To hear the story of Genesis 2—3 behind the covering of history, we must discover the text itself.

We can phrase the problem of interpretation as a question: Where do we start? We have already made one important decision by determining that we will begin with the text itself in Genesis 2—3, instead of with our own modern retellings of the story. Of course, we will produce another retelling, but at least it will be a retelling of the story itself, rather than a retelling of someone else's retelling. This is a difficult process, and this means that we will first have to be very clear about the traditional interpretation, so that we can ignore it while we concentrate on the story itself.

Within the story, where do we start? We can think in terms of characters. Who is the most important character in this story? Who is the story about? In the end, we will find that it is both a story about God and a story about people. But we must choose a place to start. The traditional interpretation starts with the assumption that the story is about God, but newer approaches have called this assumption into question.

A Traditional Interpretation

There is no single "traditional interpretation" of the story of Adam and Eve found in Genesis 2—3. The story is an intriguing and complex one. There are many layers present in the story, and so no solitary interpretation of the text has achieved complete dominance. There have been many differences between the various influential interpretations of the story. Nevertheless, there has been a tradition of interpretation. That is, most interpretations (especially those before the past twenty years) have possessed some very crucial features in common. These shared interpretive features mean that strong similarities between the different interpretations combine into one general tradition. Though there is variation in details, most readings of Genesis 2—3 have been basically the same. The similarities among the traditional interpretations appear all the more clearly when contrasted with more recent interpretations, especially those from explicitly feminist approaches.

To say, therefore, that these features of interpretation are *traditional* is to talk about who has accepted these features as truth. Age does not make something traditional; wide acceptance by certain people makes it so. In this case, the church combined with scholars and other influential religious writers to assert the truth of these basic "facts" about the text. In other words, the white male religious leaders agreed that this text meant certain things. The meaning of the text then legitimated the actions that those leaders desired and chose.

What are these basic facts about Genesis 2—3 that identify the traditional interpretations? Many of them focus on the nature and status of the woman, Eve, thus allowing the generalizations from this woman to all women. She is secondary, derivative, inferior, dependent, powerless, untrustworthy, gullible, submissive, and punished.[1] Adam, however, seems upstanding, and most of these traditional interpretations emphasize how God created Adam as the capstone of all creation and how God and Adam walked together in the garden, sharing the world together. One gains the impression that God created Adam because God needed a friend, and so God created a man who was almost perfect and then created an almost perfect garden for God's friend to inhabit. God then gave this man, the most privileged of all creation, a personal helper to assist him in his endeavors. But this secondary creation was somehow weak, and God's enemy perverted her and Adam through her, destroying the possibilities for an intimate relationship between God and Adam.[2]

In these traditional interpretations of Genesis 2—3, it is commonplace to begin with God. After all, God is the first character that the story introduces, being present from the very beginning.[3] The other characters enter only later, with God specifically involved with the creation of Adam and of Eve through the course of the narrative. Furthermore, God is the logical beginning to the

---

[1]See the list of common assumptions about Genesis 2—3 provided by Phyllis Trible, *God and the Rhetoric of Sexuality* (Overtures to Biblical Theology, 2; Philadelphia: Fortress Press, 1978), p. 73.

[2]In the retellings of the grand sweep of religious history, the next step is usually the description of how these events render all humanity unacceptable to God, a condition that changes only through Jesus Christ. The misogyny of this construction is clear: through a woman, sin comes into the world, infecting first one man and then all men, and this sin is cured by the male Jesus who never has a female partner or counterpart. Sin enters by women and is removed only by a male who rejects women.

[3]Genesis 2:4b is probably the beginning of this story.

story, because God is the first cause for what happens. For this reason, the story is termed a creation story, with the understanding that the real topic of the narrative is God's activity. God creates, God communes with the creation, God discovers a problem, and then God punishes and sentences. Always, God is concerned with God's own status and glory. When sin enters the picture, it affronts God, and so God removes the sin by removing the sinners from the garden. God is the story's main character in these traditional interpretations.

If God is the main character, then God experiences two relationships within the narrative that structure the entire plot. The first of these relationships is positive and the second is negative; together, these two connections of characters form the moral matrix that makes sense out of the story. God experiences a positive relationship with Adam. God creates Adam as the climax of creation, and Adam then enjoys a special, privileged intimacy with God. This is a large part of the idyllic quality of the paradise narrative. If there was only a perfect garden, it would not be enough to be a true paradise, but the close intimacy between God and human make this story into a tale of a religious perfection. Human and God live together in perfect harmony, with the human undertaking the appropriate work and doing it to God's satisfaction. Because of Adam's role in this perfect relationship in paradise, Adam becomes normative; this first male is the stereotypical human, and all subsequent humans should emulate Adam, even as we should do today. Maleness becomes the model for humanity.

Of course, Adam failed at one crucial test, and this ruined the relationship between God and Adam. But the traditional interpretations emphasize that the sin resulted from an intrusion into this relationship. Only when woman intervenes between God and man does sin occur, destroying the perfection of man's relationship with God. Thus, the final model for human perfection is maleness without female intervention.[4]

God's other chief relationship is with the snake. From one perspective the story moves toward a climax in which God and the snake confront each other, with God as the victor and the

---

[4]Later church traditions that insisted on the virginity of Jesus and the celibacy of priests continued this emphasis, and adherents of these notions often referred back to Genesis 2—3 and these traditional interpretations of that story in order to support their own views and practices.

snake as the loser who is not destroyed completely and so can return to fight another day.[5] Within the structure of the story, the snake and God are opposites. According to the traditional interpretation, God and the snake issue conflicting commands. God orders that humans not eat certain fruit, and the snake tells them to do it. The snake is the antithesis of God. The traditions and interpretations that identify the snake with Satan or some other evil supernatural being follow and further this line of thinking. God and Satan are eternal antagonists; God is this story's hero and Satan is the story's villain. The snake as villain works well within the structure of the story, because literary tension rises as the snake seems to gain ground against God, but in the end the hero wins, as we all knew should happen.

By this interpretation, God and snake fight against each other in a continuing cosmic war, of which one battle is fought on human turf. God has a friend, an ally in this battle—Adam. When Adam fails, God is hurt, since God must continue the fight without this ally. Had Adam been stronger, then perhaps Adam could have defeated Satan by himself, but instead, God reenters the story at the end after Adam's failure, and God reestablishes the divine order without any help from others. God ends the story quite lonely, trapped within the garden of perfection without anyone else qualified to be there. Even though God had created for companionship, God is all alone at the end. God wins, but it seems an almost empty victory; the story must be read as tragedy if God is the hero.

There is, of course, a fourth character in this story: Eve, the woman. She is on the same structural plane as the man, Adam, but possesses a very different character. God and the snake are opposites, because they each issue opposite instructions. However, there is an absolutely crucial difference: God speaks to Adam but the snake talks with Eve. Both God and the snake are persuasive. Of course Adam should obey God, but Eve sins by obeying the snake. Thus, Eve is more than Adam's counterpart. Just as Adam became God's partner in the naming of the animals, Eve becomes the snake's partner in the matter of the fruit from the tree. Eve chooses loyalty to Satan instead of obedience to God.

---

[5]In this formulation, the snake fights God when Jesus hangs on the cross; Jesus' victory crushes the snake forever. Interestingly, this theological move places Jesus as the successor to God.

    This is why the brunt of the punishment falls upon Eve. Both Eve and Adam failed to be God's ally in the cosmic battle against Satan, but Eve's failure is much worse. Whereas Adam was unsuccessful as God's ally, Eve *succeeded* as Satan's partner. Adam was not sufficiently swayed by loyalty to God, but Eve followed Satan, and believed in the snake so much that she became a virtual evangelist for Satan, converting Adam against his better knowledge and against his will to obey God and to maintain that idyllic relationship.

    For her sin, Eve receives the worst punishment. She is sentenced to a life of pain. Her role is childbearing, and she will accomplish her task only with great pain. Any avoidance of this sentence, through any lifestyle or technique that avoids pregnancy, is thus to be condemned. Furthermore, her desire will be toward her husband, even though that desire only ends in the pains of pregnancy and childbirth. Not only does she go through life in pain, but she longs for the things that bring pain. Woman should seek after pain, because only in that pain can she approach the right relationships with man and with God.

    At one level, the story is cosmic in its concerns. The context is a fight between God and Satan, and the outcome of the battle is not certain. Humans enter only as potential allies to the supernatural warring factions. Adam attempted to be loyal to God, but succumbed to female sin. The woman Eve never even tried to obey God, but instead allied herself with Satan, for whom she proved a strong and faithful ally. Because of her sin, God ejected both man and woman out of paradise and out of personal relationship with their creator, and sentenced both of them to punishment. For Eve, this meant that she would desire her own continual punishment. Adam also received punishment, but his is the tilling of the ground with hard physical labor. In the future, children could share this work with him. Because of this, he actually benefits from Eve's punishment! She labors to produce laborers who will help bear Adam's burden.

    In the end, the story is about God, and serves to explain several features of God's nature. First of all, it emphasizes God's good intentions, because God creates a paradise and gives the humans everything they need. Secondly, the story teaches us that God demands obedience, and disobedience receives swift punishment. The punishment is also severe; if one even bites into the wrong fruit, one can become cursed for life! This is because of the third point: God is in constant cosmic conflict with Satan, who will always subvert God's intentions by preying on weak humans. Lastly, the story explains why life now is so hard and why God never does anything to make life better. Things are bad because we deserve it. Life is hard, then we die. God wants it that way, and it's not God's fault. Life's impoverishment and difficulty are the humans' fault, and especially the woman's fault.

In this reading, the focus of the story is not upon the woman, but later retellings of the story increasingly emphasize the aspects that focus on Eve. Thus, there are more lessons that are taught from this text. Woman is the source of sin. Woman is inferior to man. Women are trouble. Women deserve to hurt, and they seek out pain. Women's pain is not wrong or evil; it's the way God wants things to be. These messages and so many more like them flow out from these traditional interpretations of Genesis 2—3, and these ideas have poisoned the world for thousands of years. Men, including influential religious leaders, have propagated these messages, respecting and worshiping a God who favors the pain of others, such as women. Such interpreters seem to think that God's desire to see others hurt somehow supports them in their attempts to live comfortable lives. In the face of such misuse of this story to cause pain, the need for other approaches seems clear.

A Feminist Interpretation

Within recent years, these traditional interpretations of the story in Genesis 2—3 have come under attack from scholars and persons of faith who desire a new understanding of God and God's relationship with women, and also with all humanity. The notions of a vindictive God whose severe punishments legitimate pain and abuse seem detrimental to faith, and thus these newer interpreters have sought new ways to interpret and explain the story. Their results provide new life for this ancient story.

Feminist interpretations of biblical stories often begin with a focus on the woman or women in the story.[6] In this case, these very nontraditional interpretations start by looking at Eve. This creates a very different orientation toward the entire story than

[6]For this and other related tendencies in feminist interpretation, see Katherine Doob Sakenfeld, "Feminist Uses of Biblical Materials," in *Feminist Interpretation of the Bible,* ed. Letty M. Russell (Philadelphia: Westminster Press, 1985), pp. 55–64, especially p. 57.

that offered by the traditional interpretations that start with God's acts of creation. In fact, certain feminist interpretations reverse the direction of the entire interpretative process, and thus it is not surprising that these approaches develop very different results.

Many of these interpretations begin with Eve. By starting on the human plane and not in the divine realm, interpreters can gain a very different perspective on the text. This, of course, does not deny God's role in creation or God's primacy within the created world. Rather, the decision is a literary one about how to read this narrative. In other words, what is the story about? Is it about God's creative acts or about the first, prototypical human relationships? The story may well be about both, but where do we start? The beginning point makes a difference. Since many feminist interpreters are very interested in how humans relate, they are more likely to start on the human plane. Of course, any interpretation should incorporate both human and divine realms, to the extent that each is present within the text, regardless of where the interpretation begins.

When Eve serves as the beginning for the interpretation, the story looks quite different. Some feminist interpreters insist on strict equality between the woman and the man, using the same criteria for equality that we moderns prefer. This approach can be attractive, but it is exceedingly difficult to read Genesis 2—3 as a modern text. The text's own interests are quite different from modern thoughts, and a reading of the text should honor its original contexts as much as possible. There are still inequalities within the text, though feminist approaches make it possible to name those examples of unfairness as such.

Despite the inability to eradicate inequality, feminist interpretations provide new insights about the relationship between Eve and Adam. Eve begins the story as God's creation; she is God's final, ultimate creative act. Her very name means "life" and she brings a vibrancy to the whole world that she inhabits. Before her arrival, Adam was lonely. God's companionship was never Adam's goal; he needed human company. The story makes the point quite clearly. Eve's story begins with God's assertion: "It is not good for the earthling to be alone. I will make for it an equal companion" (Genesis 2:18).[7]

---

[7]All translations of scripture are the author's.

Other translations render this as a search for a helper, perhaps implying in English some sort of subservient relationship.[8]
This has resulted in the notion that God thinks Adam needs a
servant, and so gives him a wife. But that is not the picture at all.
God shows all of the animals to Adam, and Adam realizes that
none of these would be an equal companion. Adam does not
need a slave or a trained beast; this earthling needs someone
else with whom to talk and share life. God deigns to create
another being that is like Adam, so that there will be companionship. This requires equality and mutuality.[9] The two earthlings
would share the same tasks and the same responsibilities, and
would live in a mutually fulfilling relationship of support and
enrichment.

The woman, then, finds her being as one who is equal to
Adam, like the man ("flesh of his flesh," according to Genesis
2:23) and a companion with him. Since she shares companionship with him in helpful ways, it is sensible that she also shares
his work. Together they will do what God requires. Eve is every
bit as human as Adam, and in God's sight they are equal creations, sharing the same functions and responsibilities.

Eve also possesses moral reasoning and independent judgment, which should certainly be understood as high virtues. For
many feminist interpreters, this is the import of Eve's conversation with the snake. She shows that she understands the issues at
stake. Eve responds to the snake's questions with knowledge of
what God said, but soon the snake's questioning goes beyond
what Eve knows. Then, she discovers that the fruit seems good to
eat, and that it would increase wisdom (Genesis 3:6). Eve's
mistake, of course, comes in trusting the snake, but she knew
what the narrator had already said: the snake was one of God's
cleverest creatures (Genesis 3:1), and so there was good reason
for that trust. To be honest, the snake was perfectly right. The
fruit did increase Eve's knowledge, and she did not die that day.
At best, we could say that Eve was right; she saw the fruit,
evaluated it correctly, and ate in order to gain knowledge, a

---

[8]The Hebrew term often translated as "helper" does carry a connotation
of assistance, but whether the help comes from a superior or an inferior
cannot be determined without context. This term, describing what the
woman does for Adam, can also refer to what God does for the people
(Psalms 33:20; 54:4; 70:5; 79:9; 109:26; 115:9–11). Clearly, this kind of
"help" does not denote servitude or subservience.

[9]See Trible, *God and the Rhetoric of Sexuality*, p. 90.

worthwhile goal. The worst valuation would be that Eve made a mistake, but it was an error made with good thinking behind it; we might call it an honest mistake. The man has the same information at his disposal and makes the same decision. If there is blame at this action, it belongs not to one or the other in varying degrees but to both woman and man equally.

When one compares Eve and Adam, the contrast is apparent. Both make the same decision and take the same action based on the same knowledge. In that, they are identical. But Eve seems the active one throughout. We readers never know why Adam ate; Eve at least has reasons that seem solid, even if mistaken. She can conduct theological argumentation and moral reasoning, and thus Adam has no difficulty when she acts as the speaker for the couple. He remains silent; she speaks of God and God's commands.[10]

When they appear before Yahweh facing questions about their deeds, Adam immediately blames Eve, claiming that she made him do it. But Adam's accusations do not stop there. He continues to blame even God, for it was God who gave the woman to him. Adam claims that the disobedience was, at root, God's fault. This is certainly more of a distortion of God's words, deeds, and intentions than the snake had committed.[11] Eve, on the other hand, admits her complicity more quickly, though she claims that the snake deceived her.

After the questioning, God announces reality. By this interpretation, God does not punish the humans; God simply states what is and what will be. Though God clearly curses the snake, the terminology for cursing or punishment is absent from God's statements to the humans. These statements require close attention.

> To the woman, God said: "I will greatly multiply your handiwork and your pregnancy. With work, you can bear children. Your sexual attraction is toward your own man; he will be likewise to you."

> To the earthling, God said: "You have heard the sound of your wife. She ate from the tree about which I had instructed you, 'You should not eat from it.' Cursed is the

---

[10]For a more extensive development of the material in this paragraph, see Trible, *God and the Rhetoric of Sexuality*, pp. 110–114. One should also note Adam's silence throughout the discussion with the snake; it forms a striking contrast with the silence of the women in this book's next chapter.

[11]Trible, *God and the Rhetoric of Sexuality*, p. 119.

earth because of you. With handiwork you will eat of it all
the days of your life. The earth will sprout thorns and
thistles for you; you will eat the grass of the pastures.
With sweat dripping off your nose, you will eat bread, until
you return to the earth, because you were taken from it.
Because you were soil, to soil will you return."

Genesis 3:16–19

God explains to the two humans what their life will be like.
Though there is no curse, they will live lives of work. For the
woman, she will have more work with her hands and more
pregnancy. Both are means of productivity, and Yahweh will
bless her with both opportunities to contribute to life. For the
man, there is only one way to contribute: work with the hands,
which means the back-breaking work in the fields. His work will
be difficult because his actions have caused the earth to be
cursed. Neither the man nor the woman receive any direct
punishment, but God gives both of them tasks to do with their
lives, just as Adam had a task before Eve's arrival. Both have a
place within the created world, and both have complementary
work to do. Neither is less than the other; disobedience has diminished them both and new knowledge has enhanced them both.

Throughout this type of feminist interpretation, God receives
little direct attention. Truly, this interpretation depicts a story that
is about humans and their interrelations in God's presence, rather
than a story about God *per se*. By beginning with Eve and Adam,
this interpretation shows that God reacts rather than acts throughout the story. When Adam is lonely, God creates; when the
humans disobey, God enters to ask questions and state destinies.
This agrees with a God who desires the humans to possess the
powers of moral choice and who is willing to leave them alone to
the degree necessary to allow those choices. God does not
intervene to prevent the eating of that fruit; God comes around
later without seeming to know what had happened. God allows
the humans to develop in the directions of their choosing, waiting
to see what will happen and then acting after the fact in reaction
to human activity. God is passive and often absent, but still
interested and involved.

This speaks of a very different experience of God than that
spoken by the interpretations that emphasize God's creative acts
within the story. In those lines of thought, God sets this up in
active, creative ways. Of course, the experiences of God as
present and as absent are *both* Old Testament notions; neither is

heretical and both represent a reality of life in relationship with God. The question here deals with what elements of that communion receive the emphasis. By the feminist interpretations, Genesis 2—3 is not a story about God's creation; it is a story about human relationships and responsibilities, much like the later parts of the book of Genesis and many other parts of the Bible. The moral, ethical, and social dimensions rise to prominence, giving direction about how humans should act at all times. Of course, the answer in the early parts of the story is obedience and the end's answer is hard work. Both inescapably point to God as the source of instruction and as the provider of relevant work. Moral discussions soon turn back to theological discourse.

Problems with Feminist Interpretations

The feminist interpretation developed above avoids some of the problems of traditional interpretations, especially regarding the more severe misogynies that blame women for sin and separation from God.[12] Certainly, the story in Genesis 2—3 talks about disobedience and isolation on the part of both humans. But these feminist interpretations are not without their own problems. Perhaps these problems are solvable, but they seem to be ignored more than they should be.

The first of these problems is the role of the snake. In feminist interpretations, God's role decreases, but the role of the snake virtually disappears. This is, of course, both good and bad. The text never claims that the snake is supernatural; this talking snake surprises no one at all. When God curses the snake, God expects that this is a purely natural, normal creature, not Satan incarnate. But the snake is a striking feature of the story, for us readers if not for the characters themselves. The snake needs further explanation.

Along with the problem of the snake, we need to address the problem of disobedience. Traditional interpretations emphasized the entry of sin into the world and the "Fall of Man." This was overdone; the story itself never mentions sin by name or an equivalent. Any notion of a "fall from grace" depends on other texts and extrabiblical theology; we cannot derive or deduce the fall from these two chapters of Genesis. Still, the feminist inter-

---

[12]Of course, the interpretation offered above is only one possible feminist interpretation, and it certainly does not exhaust all the options, even though it is representative of several prominent current interpretations.

pretations often cannot find anything in this story that is *wrong*. People go through life making decisions as best they know how, and then God explains their future mode of existence, but there is no sin and no real problems. But the story does seem to state that there are problems. At the end, the humans are gone from paradise. That may not be so bad; perhaps humans are supposed to be in the world and hard at work. But the humans leave alienated from God and isolated from each other, and that is clearly wrong. Our interpretations should have a sense of what went wrong and what should have been done instead, without resorting to blaming.

This story of Eve and Adam is clearly a moral story, and we readers should draw moral conclusions from it. We should learn what to do and what not to do; we should figure out how to make moral decisions in a complex and confusing world. Regardless of the particular interpretative stance, this need to make moral decisions should come through this text. Does knowledge help us make better decisions or does knowledge hinder moral activity? Is the search for knowledge moral or immoral, or neither? Does God require blind obedience, or informed decision making, or simply that we know the choices before rigid obedience? Does disobedience lead to physical death or to some other lack? Is physical labor punishment or is it the expression of life in partnership with God? These questions reside right underneath the surface of the text, and these questions need answers.

Toward a New Interpretation

Both the traditional and feminist interpretations give only limited attention to one major character within this story: the earth. The earth is prominent throughout the story. In a striking sense, this is the story not of God's creation nor of human relationships, but of the *earth's* fall from grace. The story begins while God is creating the earth (Genesis 2:4b) and ends with the cursing of the earth—though the earth had done nothing wrong at all (Genesis 3:17). In the meantime, God creates creatures from the earth, and calls them earthlings. The story even explains that the earthling's purpose is to serve the earth—not self or God (Genesis 2:5). At the story's beginning, Yahweh makes the earth grow bountiful good things (Genesis 2:9), but at the end, the earthling tends the earth and makes things grow with much hard work (Genesis 3:18). Of course, it is not at all surprising that it takes much human effort to equal what Yahweh was doing beforehand. In the end, the woman returns to the man from which she came, and the earthlings will return to the earth, from which they came. Earth surrounds the story.

This presents a new possibility for the purpose of creation. God desires humans (and animals, also) to tend the earth. Caring for the earth and making things grow was at first God's work, but now God seeks helpers, like the man and the woman, to serve the earth. This removes some of the responsibility from God's shoulders, but it also creates a cooperative project for humanity and divinity to perform together. The purpose of creation is the care of the earth. For this reason, human life comes out of the earth and returns to the earth at the end of life. Our purpose is the care of the earth. Why then was the earth created? These chapters never discuss that, but it might not be too outlandish to suggest that it gives us—both humans and God—something to do and, more importantly, something to do *together*.

This may give us a clue about the meaning of the whole first section of the book of Genesis. Through the many stories, humanity slowly expands to fill the whole earth. Many scholars have talked about this as a theme of scattering.[13] Often, this dispersion receives a negative interpretation; it is the result of sin and a symptom of increasing alienation. But perhaps this reading is wrong. If the purpose of humanity is to serve the earth, then the fulfillment of this purpose requires that God distribute humanity throughout the earth. After all, humans cannot be effective servants in places where they are not present.

This positive, purposive dispersion requires also an increase in the human population. One human, Adam, could not tend the whole earth. For this reason, God created Eve as an equal companion to the man. However, God was not naive; there was no thought that two humans could tend the whole earth any better than one could. What Eve and Adam could do together, in addition to tending their part of the earth, was to procreate. Through an expanding population that continued their outward motion to the ends of the earth, God enabled humanity to attain their purpose, which is the service of the whole earth. Of course, one may judge how well we succeed and express that judgment with somber evaluation.

---

[13]For example, see Gerhard von Rad, *Old Testament Theology: Volume I* (New York: Harper and Row, 1962), pp. 158, 163.

Eve's Story

Thus, Eve's story is one of partnership, with God and with man. Together, their effort consists of hard work to serve the earth. For Eve, this work takes two forms. There is the work of the hands, which serves the earth directly. Eve and Adam share this work, and in this labor they are partners and coworkers. Eve has another task as well: pregnancy and childbirth. God blesses these dangerous tasks, because they too serve the earth, though indirectly through the production of the next generation of laborers.

Probably, the story in Genesis 2—3 reached its present form in the early years of the Israelite monarchy, under King David or King Solomon. For these people, the story would have had a special significance. As discussed in the previous chapter, life changed in the first years of the monarchy. In early Israel, before the rise of kings, men and women had worked in the fields as equals until an economic, agricultural crisis required that the Israelites increase their population to provide more workers for the labor-intensive work of growing crops. In those days, women had two tasks: field work and childbearing. Both were absolutely necessary for the survival of the Israelite community.

When Israel gained kings, the nation gained wealth and also gained control of the cities that had previously been Canaanite. With easier farming in the valley areas around these cities, women's field labor was no longer as necessary as it had been. The tendency among the leaders at that point may have been the repression of women, telling them to stay at home and do "women's work," especially procreation. This would have allowed the male leaders to enhance their own power and privilege through the control of their own families. But some people argued against this reduction in women's roles. This story of Eve and Adam might have been important proof for these protestors who favored women's right to work in the fields. Humanity's purpose, shared by both men and women, is the service of the earth.

Of course, women have another task, childbearing; God intends women to do both. Only women have the ability to do both. Any human effort to limit women into only one role violated God's intentions, as expressed in Genesis 2—3. Thus this story of humanity's origins as servants of the earth had immediate political importance as well as enduring theological and moral implications.

Chapter 4

Silence

The relationship of all people to the land continues in the stories of Sarah, Hagar, Rebekah, and Sarah's nameless niece. These stories from the middle of the book of Genesis focus on two generations of humanity's dispersion. Already there are humans throughout the world; the twin events of the flood and Babel guarantee that the humans scattered to the ends of the earth. Still, the chief concern is population for the land. The community must produce enough people to take care of the land. There is safety in numbers throughout this story, and there is also wealth in numbers. When population is low, however, then famine threatens once more. Hunger awaits those who do not multiply their numbers, though God blesses with plentiful food those who increase the population. This represents the experience of the Israelites in the years just before the monarchy, and probably in many of the rural areas well into the monarchic period.

The previous two chapters developed the thesis that women's roles receded in the early monarchy, shifting from an emphasis on cooperation with men in the general roles of society (primarily agricultural) to an emphasis on childbearing. Through the early Israelite period, before the monarchy, crisis triggered the need for population increase, but the monarchic period transformed these social changes from temporary emergency measures to permanent, established features of Israelite religion and culture.[1] These texts from the middle of Genesis support and further this thesis. These four women have very little involvement in agriculture, and truly their roles outside the home are extremely limited. Pregnancy and childbirth, however, are dominant features of these stories, and it is not accidental that these women, as a group, are most remembered for the male children they bear.

One other reality marks these women. They are silent. Of course, they speak from time to time; they are not mute. When in public, though, the men around them expect these women to stay silent. The women may speak in private to the men, but even then the men do not always listen. Eve lived in a world where women spoke their minds. She spoke for herself and for Adam, and he showed no displeasure in allowing her to speak for him in public. Furthermore, Eve engaged in theological discourse, and she spoke with God, verbally claiming responsibility for her actions. How different things are for these women in the middle of Genesis! The repression of their roles reflects itself in the restriction of their speech. These women's silence points to their true stories of loss and reduction, even though they rarely speak to tell us those stories.

For these women, Sarah fills the role of mother. However, the role is figurative in all three cases. Sarah is Hagar's mistress and ruler, Rebekah's mother-in-law, and the aunt to the unnamed woman who married Abraham's nephew, Lot. Sarah appears as silent, and that silence echoes throughout these other women's stories. Not only is she silent, but she allows men to speak for her, and men's speech proves consistently dangerous. All of these women face danger, and almost always their pain, loss, and victimization has its roots in men's speech.

Sarah's Silence

The Ancestress Endangered

Sarah's story contains one episode twice in virtually identical forms with different villains. In Genesis 12:10–20, Abram and Sarai (the earlier names for Abraham and Sarah) journey to Egypt because there was a famine in their own land and they

---

[1]For a more extensive development of a closely related thesis, see Carol Meyers, *Discovering Eve: Ancient Israelite Women in Context* (Oxford: Oxford University Press, 1988), especially pp. 189–196.

needed food. But Abram worries that Sarai's beauty will attract the attention of Pharaoh, Egypt's ruler, and that Pharaoh will murder Abram in order to possess Sarai. So Abram develops a plan. He will lie to Pharaoh, denying that Sarai is his wife. Then, Pharaoh can sleep with Sarai without endangering Abram. But God punishes Pharaoh for this sin of adultery, and Pharaoh realizes his mistake. He gives Sarai back to Abram and sends them out of Egypt with enough wealth to have made the visit and the ruse quite profitable. In Genesis 20:1–18, the same basic plot repeats itself. In the second story, Abraham's opponent is Abimelech, the King of Gerar. Again, Abraham profited from the lie, but God cursed Abimelech and his family.

For Abraham, the ruse is protective. At the price of a lie, he guarantees his own safety, and he gains much more than that. Through these situations, he becomes wealthy and powerful. He stands up to Pharaoh and to Abimelech, and he backs them down. These great kings end up giving Abraham gifts to pay him and to appease him. Abraham is seen to be clever and tricky, which were characteristics that the ancient Israelites considered virtuous.[2] Abraham gains respect in the minds of ancient readers by proving that he can outthink and outtrick even great rulers of important nations. Not only does the ruse protect Abraham, but it gives him wealth in his present and respect for posterity. Of course, this comes at the expense of kings of other nations, but that only makes the story juicier.

Sarah, however, faces real danger at the hands of these kings. For her the ruse means rape and abuse, along with humiliation and isolation. In the face of such possibilities, she remains silent.

The True Threat to Sarah

The tension in this plot runs much deeper than that, however. Sarah is more than the noble woman who remains silent in the face of her own victimization. Her husband sells her sexual services for money and personal advantage. Abraham is a pimp and he makes a whore out of his own wife, for his own financial benefit. According to Abraham's telling of the story, Pharaoh and

---

[2]For a detailed discussion of the virtue of trickery in ancient Israelite literature, see Susan Niditch, *Underdogs and Tricksters: A Prelude to Biblical Folklore* (San Francisco: Harper and Row, 1987).

Abimelech represent real threats to Abraham's safety. Abraham then endangers his own wife to protect himself.

Abraham is more than a wily, greedy trickster here. He goes far beyond any boundaries of decency to sell his own wife into sexual slavery. His untruths, perhaps a defensible part of the trickery by themselves, threaten Sarah's very life in order to protect his own safety. He offers false witness that damages his wife and his neighbors the kings.[3] Abraham claims that these other kings endanger him, and then the narrative points to the danger the kings pose to Sarah. Abraham himself is the true danger, to himself through the loss of his truthfulness and to the kings who receive punishment and loss because of Abraham's trickery. Abraham is the true danger to Sarah, because he sells her to protect himself.

The Reward at the End

At the end of each of these short episodes within Sarah's story, there is reward. Sure, the road has been rough and sacrifices were made by all, Abraham might argue, but everything worked out all right in the end, didn't it? Abraham certainly receives rewards that can be counted, as these two kings give him money to make him rich. But what does Sarah receive for her sacrifice? It is hard to see that she receives anything.

The larger story does move on though. If it is right that the overarching purpose of these stories is to tend for the land, then Sarah's death is a key part of that overall narrative progression. When Sarah dies at an old age, Abraham negotiates for the purchase of a plot of land in which to bury her (Genesis 23:1–20). The significance is that Sarah becomes the first occasion for the permanent acquisition of land, and it is land that becomes so important throughout this story. She returns to the ground and becomes the people's first tie to that land. If this story comes from a time when women's connections to the land were questioned by other voices in society, then this story offers a powerful message: women belong to the land, too. This might be Sarah's reward—the opportunity to occupy the land. But as such it is an

---

[3]Compare Exodus 20:16. Lies that intend to damage others are strictly forbidden by Israelite law. See Walter Harrelson, *The Ten Commandments and Human Rights* (Overtures to Biblical Theology, 8; Philadelphia: Fortress Press, 1980), pp. 143–148.

exceedingly poor reward. Though it helps the progression of the story, it does Sarah very little good at all, since she has already died. A decent burial hardly atones for repeated episodes of rape and abuse by foreign kings at her own husband's behest.

The Test

Perhaps the best known of Abraham's stories comes in Genesis 22, when God commands Abraham to take his only son, Isaac, up to the top of a mountain, where Abraham would sacrifice Isaac to God. Abraham obeys, but God intervenes at the last possible moment to save the child. This testing of Abraham is one of the most striking narratives within the entire Bible, and creates a stark picture of the price of faith.[4] But what happens to Sarah during this story? Isaac is her son, too; why should she be absent from her husband's sacrifice of her son? Not only is she silent, but she is completely absent, and her absence begins the story's own critique of itself.

The story is strange in that it starts out with a clear statement to the reader: this is a test. God tested Abraham. But Abraham never seems to know this; God never mentions the fact that this is a test to Abraham. We know who is testing whom, but what, precisely, is the test? According to the standard, traditional interpretations, God tests Abraham to see if he really trusts God. If Abraham does trust God, then Abraham will choose to murder his only son Isaac at God's command, even though God had promised Abraham that his future was tied to the boy Isaac (Genesis 21:12). The test expects that Abraham should trust and obey God, despite how things look on the human level, according to this interpretation.[5]

However, this interpretation seems to be an oversimplification of a very tricky problem. The story itself, within the larger context of the Abraham stories, produces a conflict of logical impossibility. On the one hand, God tells Abraham that Isaac is essential to the future that God has promised. To kill Isaac for any reason would be a violation of the covenants that God had already made with Abraham. Isaac's death negates God's prom-

---

[4]For a detailed analysis of the story, see James L. Crenshaw, *A Whirlpool of Torment: Israelite Traditions of God as an Oppressive Presence* (Overtures to Biblical Theology 12; Philadelphia: Fortress Press, 1984).

[5]Of course, later traditions about the meaning of God's role in Christ's death have shaped the interpretation of this story.

ises about Isaac. On the other hand, God now gives Abraham a clear command: sacrifice Isaac. Abraham should obey God's commands, because that demonstrates faith in God. Thus, Abraham faces a logical dilemma; both paths are required and yet either path is wrong. What should he do?

There is a solution to the dilemma, but it becomes visible only when one reads the chapters leading up to Genesis 22. One of our assumptions is wrong, and so there really is no dilemma; Abraham's choice should be clear to him. Our wrong assumption deals with what it means to obey God. In our thinking, informed by the traditional histories and retellings, obedience means doing exactly what God says. We should follow God's commands to the letter, without questioning; that is faith, or so we are told. But this is not the Old Testament's understanding of what close relationships with God are all about. One only has to look at Abraham and Sarah to see this.

God discusses proper action in Genesis 18:19. God desires that God's people perform justice and righteousness. God does not require obedience in our understanding of the term; God requires right action. There can be quite a difference. This statement by God introduces a discussion between God and Abraham dealing with the impending destruction of Sodom and Gomorrah. God states the divine intention, and then Abraham does the right thing: *he argues.* Abraham argues with God and changes God's mind. Humans can change God's mind and teach God to do the right thing.[6] That is the relationship God desires. Argumentation with God is not a bad thing. Just as when Eve discusses theology with the snake and when Sarah questions God about the reality of a coming child in old age, God desires discussion. Abraham knew this in Genesis 18, but he forgets it in Genesis 22.

Therefore, there is no dilemma. It only seems a dilemma when we insist on a literal obedience instead of a personal relationship with God. God tested Abraham, and Abraham should have questioned and argued. Abraham should have reminded God about God's own promises. But instead Abraham chooses silence, which was the wrong choice. For this reason, God intervenes at the last minute. God gave Abraham all the time to figure

---

[6]Moses also argues with God and convinces God to save lives (Exodus 32:9–14); Moses specifically mentions the promises to Abraham and Isaac as reasons that God should not kill the Israelites.

out the test, but that didn't happen, and so God had to intervene or risk losing precious Isaac. Abraham failed the test.

Often modern interpreters phrase the test as an investigation of Abraham's belief in God's power. Does this human believe that God will intervene at the last minute? Does Abraham think that God has that ability? Such an interpretation, however, proves to be most unsatisfactory. If that is the case, then Abraham is testing God, by seeing how far he can go to kill his own son before God steps in to prevent this evil deed. God did not ask Abraham to do wrong, and there is no proof of human faith in undertaking a wrong act just to see if God will intervene.[7] Such would be Abraham testing God, instead of the opposite. Abraham's desire to murder Isaac is wrong, and it demonstrates his failure to understand what God is doing. He fails the test.

If Abraham had only involved Sarah, things might have been different. Sarah was willing to argue with God (Genesis 18:12, 15). She understood the importance of life and God's desire that we live it fully in relationship with God—working toward the promises, not against them. Sarah might have broken the silence and spoken in ways that would have saved Abraham from his error. But he never asked her. Abraham did nothing to bring Sarah into the situation, even though her investment was as great as his and, more importantly, she might well have solved the test correctly. Abraham aided Sarah in silence by not asking her, and that silence resulted in Abraham's failure.

This story brings silence. It brings silence to Sarah, who never speaks again. It kills the relationship between Abraham and Sarah; he shows no intimacy toward her until after her death. It silences the relationship between Abraham and Isaac, since they never face each other again. It even ends the relationship between God and Abraham, who never speak to each other again. All of this rich matrix of intimacy falls apart, leaving only silence in its wake.

The Dangerous Ancestor and His Silent Wife

Abraham is dangerous. His selfishness endangers Sarah more than once by subjecting her to sexual slavery. He creates catastrophe for neighboring kings. He tries to murder his own son. He fails God's test. Disaster surrounds him on all sides.

---

[7]"Should we sin more so that grace will abound? By no means!" (Romans 6:1–2).

Much of his danger arises from his desire for a silent wife. If he would have allowed Sarah's speech, perhaps things would have been different. She would have avoided the charades with Pharaoh and Abimelech. Perhaps she would have argued further with God to save others in Sodom and Gomorrah. Almost certainly she would have argued with God to save her son, helping Abraham to pass the test.

Through it all, Sarah remains silent. She does not object when her husband sells her twice into sexual slavery.[8] She is not allowed to speak at any of the important turning points of her life with her husband. At the end, she receives as her only reward the silence of the grave. Silence, it seems, is death.

Hagar's Silence

This sympathetic portrayal of Sarah ignores her relationship to her maid, Hagar. When Sarah speaks to and about Hagar, her speech turns destructive.[9] But this does not contradict the hopes for Sarah's speech as discussed above, because there is one correctable problem with Sarah's speech: she tries to silence Hagar through exile. Faced with her own imposed silence, Sarah desires other women to be silent as well. But silence always leads to destruction. It is not just Sarah's silence that destroys the life God intends; any woman's forced silence undoes a bit of creation.

Sarah's Idea

Sarah had a problem, and that problem motivated an attempt at a solution. Sarah's problem was that she was barren. As the society moved increasingly to emphasize childbirth as women's only possible contribution of significance, infertility took on larger

---

[8]Abimelech reports hearing her support Abraham's lie (Genesis 20:5), but Sarah never speaks out loud in either text.

[9]An excellent discussion of the Hagar stories appears in Phyllis Trible, *Texts of Terror: Literary-Feminist Readings of Biblical Narratives* (Overtures to Biblical Theology, 13; Philadelphia: Fortress Press, 1984), pp. 9–35. A marvelously effective and affective interpretation of the story can be found in Renita J. Weems, *Just a Sister Away: A Womanist Vision of Women's Relationships in the Bible* (San Diego, California: LuraMedia, 1988), pp. 1–21. For a much more extensive feminist treatment of Hagar, see Savina J. Teubal, *Hagar the Egyptian: The Lost Traditions of the Matriarchs* (San Francisco: Harper and Row, 1990).

and larger proportions of painfulness. The society's evaluation of Sarah's problem as one of the worst things in the world that could ever happen drove Sarah to ponder other solutions. Then, she had an idea (Genesis 16). She would give a slave to Abraham. Just as Abraham had sold his wife Sarah into sexual slavery with Pharaoh and Abimelech, Sarah would sell her slave into sexual union with her husband. The symmetry is amazing, but the repetition of this wrongful slavery promises no good. Sarah intended to do to Hagar the same evil silencing that was done to her.

The evil only increased. Once Hagar produced the desired offspring, it only made matters worse. Sarah insisted that Abraham send Hagar and the son away (Genesis 16:5–6). Though Hagar is back with the family later, having survived by the grace of God, Sarah once more wishes Hagar to be gone (Genesis 21:8–14). It is not enough for Sarah to debase her slave through controlling her reproduction; Sarah wants Hagar out of her sight. Furthermore, Sarah may have more than isolation in mind. She may be suggesting exposure, which was an ancient practice of terminating an unwanted child's life by leaving it outside the village, where it would die by neglect. If this is on Sarah's mind, then she also desires the death of Hagar by the same means, a particularly cruel atrocity. Regardless of Sarah's precise thoughts, her cruelty is clear.

Distance and Silence

Sarah desires distance between herself and Hagar, and the silence prefigures that distance. Sarah forces complete silence upon Hagar; the slave speaks only once, and her son never.[10] Sarah's voice fills the air, leaving hardly any room for other voices, and Hagar and Ishmael never break through the silence that Sarah assigns them.[11]

Abraham does speak in this passage (Genesis 16:6), but his comment is quite brief: "Your servant-girl belongs to you; do to her what seems good to you." Abraham avoids any strength in his voice. He could have asserted rights of ownership, since all

---

[10]See Genesis 21:16.

[11]One must be careful to avoid thinking of Sarah as shrill or petty. For a helpful review of the scholarly biases that portray Sarah and Hagar as trivially contentious women bickering around Abraham, see Jo Ann Hackett, "Rehabilitating Hagar: Fragments of an Epic Pattern," in *Gender and Difference in Ancient Israel,* ed. Peggy L. Day (Minneapolis: Fortress Press, 1989), pp. 12–27, especially pp. 12–14.

that his wife owned truly belonged to him. He could have inserted moral and ethical claims upon the situation, encouraging Sarah to do the right thing. But Abraham fails to argue Sarah into right action, just as he will fail with God regarding Isaac. Abraham's thin voice carries no weight at all; he simply echoes what he hears from Sarah without investing any of his self into his voice.

Then Sarah sends Hagar and little Ishmael away, and distance makes the silence permanent. Even if one would speak, they would be too far apart to hear each other. Distance is the strongest silence, but even before the sending, the silence was stronger than the greatest distance. The one crying in the wilderness is never heard, especially when others try not to hear.

God Speaks

One vibrant, vital voice enters into the situation to provide salvation. God speaks to Hagar through a messenger (Genesis 16:7-12; 21:17-18). The message begins in the most depressing tones; God's messenger tells Hagar to return to Sarah and to submit to her (Genesis 16:9). This means that Hagar will return to the abuse and humiliation as her superior attempts to assert privilege over her constantly. But the message continues, and there is blessing and life for Hagar and Ishmael (Genesis 16:10-11; 21:18). Again, there will be reward at the end of the story, but it is a reward that comes too late. In this life, Hagar experiences ridicule and abuse, but long after she is gone she will be the mother of her own people. Hagar eventually rises to equality with Sarah, but not until posterity, in the sweet bye and bye. Within this life on earth, there is no salvation.

Silence has taken hold of young Hagar, and it will not let go. God breaks the silence for brief moments, but even God's voice does not linger under the stifling weight of still, empty air devoid of sound. The terribly high cost of Sarah's insistence on silence comes into sharp focus; silence does bring death, even while Hagar lives.

Sarah and Hagar contrast and yet complement each other. They contest each other for power and prestige, until Hagar is forced outside, giving a powerful illustration of woman's inhumanity to woman. Had they come together, they might have empowered each other's speech, striving toward effectiveness in averting the disasters surrounding them in Abraham's household. Instead, they remained silent, using the silences against each other. The entire situation proves dysfunctional. Silence begets silence and abuse begets abuse; both reinforce the other. However, despite the repeated, continuing inhumanity of silence, God's presence is there with Hagar and her son, Ishmael.

Sarah's Niece's Silence

Perhaps Sarah had a chance to know one of her relatives. Abraham had a nephew, Lot, who had traveled with him and Sarah from Mesopotamia. For a few years, they had all stayed together, but then Abraham's family and Lot went in separate directions. These early stories (Genesis 12—13) do not mention whether or not Lot had married yet, but perhaps Sarah knew her niece, Lot's wife, from other times.

Very little is known about Sarah's niece. The stories never even mention her name. We know her two daughters and we know her husband and their hometown, Sodom, but that is almost all.

God destroyed Sodom and its neighboring towns because of their sin; we never know what those sins were. Abraham bargained with God for the life of the city, but he lapsed into silence before he had convinced God to save the city. God did send messengers to get Lot and the family out of town before the destruction, but Sarah's niece made the mistake of looking back on her way out of town. Whether this was an accident or an instant of nostalgia cannot be known; the story gives no reasons. Whatever the cause, the punishment seems overly severe; Sarah's niece became a pillar of salt. Frozen in place, we never hear her story nor any of her goals or purposes. Who was she? We never know because we never hear her story. She is frozen in stone, another woman permanently silenced.[12]

Rebekah's Silence

Sarah never met her daughter-in-law, Rebekah. This may have been for the better, because Rebekah seems to avoid the

---

[12]Renita Weems, *Just a Sister Away,* pp. 129–140, offers a thoroughly haunting retelling of this story from the viewpoint of the nameless mother of the two girls. Other information on the daughters is provided by Sharon Pace Jeansonne, *The Women of Genesis: From Sarah to Potiphar's Wife* (Minneapolis: Fortress Press, 1990), pp. 31–42.

deep-seated problems of silence that plagued Sarah and others around her. Rebekah enters the tale after Abraham's failed test had alienated him from his son, Isaac. Abraham is not willing to abandon his son to fate, even though he had been willing to murder him, and so Abraham sends a servant to seek out a suitable spouse for Isaac. That servant locates Rebekah, and then the sound of speech erupts from the vast silences of these stories.

The servant is a man of prayer, and he sets up a scene at a well so that he can judge the right woman for Isaac (Genesis 24:12–14). While still praying, Rebekah approaches the well and meets this man, who asks for a small sip of water. Immediately, she provides him with water, and then offers water for the thirsty camels as well. At first meeting, she is not only responding to this stranger but raising her voice to offer more than he desires and to initiate new levels of conversation and relationship. She speaks! Then the servant sits for a while in silence, amazed at what he has found (Genesis 24:21). In remarkable contrast to Sarah's other relatives and colleagues, Rebekah speaks, and her speech leaves men speechless.

Throughout the rest of her speaking, Rebekah takes the initiative and makes decisions that might otherwise be left for men to decide. She offers lodging to the stranger, usurping her brother's right and responsibility as the man of the house to offer hospitality to visitors (Genesis 24:25). When the men cannot decide if Rebekah should accept the offer of marriage to Isaac, they ask Rebekah, and she makes the decision herself in no uncertain terms (Genesis 24:58). Her speech controls the events; her story shapes the history.

Her voice rings out once more in a later part of her story. Rebekah mothered the twins, Esau and Jacob. By the end of his life, Isaac was blind and somewhat debilitated; he could not see the situation at hand. In Rebekah's mind, Jacob was clearly the one who should inherit the promise and the responsibility that had come down from Sarah and Abraham, but Esau was the older son by mere seconds. Rebekah then engineered Jacob's actions to secure the birthright and to become the heir of Isaac (Genesis 27:1–29). Through her deeds and the effective words of her inventive voice, Rebekah controls the situation and continues the lineage of God's chosen people in the correct direction.

Rebekah's speech allows her a blessed life and spreads blessing to those around her. For her lifetime, the stifling silence lifted like a fog burned away by the bright, illuminating sun. Happiness and the progression of God's desires await the woman who speaks and breaks the silence assigned to women.

When All the World Is Silent

By the end of these stories, the silence is deafening. Yet we cannot afford to stop our ears against the onslaught of these stories; we must listen to them attentively to hear their silent pain and their painful silence. Sarah's silence forced away her husband, her son, her purity, her joy. Hagar's silence endangered her own life and her son. Together, these women's silence, and Sarah's silencing speech, create a troubled household and a confused world. Even worse, Sarah's lack of speech fails to save Abraham (not to mention Isaac) at the moment of his most important test, which he then fails. Perhaps Sarah never knew love after Abraham sold her into sexual slavery and after she silently accepted her plight, but if she did, she never gave it voice, and her world filled with hateful, painful silence. Likewise, Sarah's niece lost her life and her whole story, immortalized for all to see in a pillar of permanent silence.

Rebekah breaks the women's silence, at least for a while. Her voice gives life and security; her speech leads others in the way of God's goals. Speech soothes away the pains of silence, but the silence has left many scars that do not go away easily.

Chapter **5**

Women Bought
and Sold

Ancient Israel did not always treat women well. In fact, through most of Israel's history women lacked so many of the common human rights that were accorded to men that women functioned almost as objects. They could be bought and sold, like animals or land or any other personal property.

To be fair, Israel was not any more severe with these laws about women than other contemporary cultures were. In fact, Israel may have had stricter laws protecting women than many other nations did. Israel's treatment of women was part of a larger system of human rights, and we moderns would find many parts of that system to be repulsive. Slavery was commonplace and almost universally accepted. Slaves, both men and women, had very limited rights, and could be bought and sold as could objects and property. The entire legal system was inherently classist. Those who had money and property had more rights than others, and movement between classes was rather limited. Israel grappled with these customs and laws and the conflict that they generated with Israel's faith, in which there was a God who cares for all the people. Israel's God, Yahweh, was much more egalitarian than the culture was, and Israel struggled to find ways to fit its faith and its culture together.

A helpful example is the familiar law about "an eye for an eye and a tooth for a tooth" (Exodus 21:24; Leviticus 24:20). Typically, we understand this as a license to violent revenge, and we then reflect on Jesus' statement: "You have heard how it was said, 'an eye for an eye and a tooth for a tooth,' but I say to you, do not resist such evil. If someone hits you on your right cheek, turn to that one the other also" (Matthew 5:38–39).[1] Jesus tells those hearing that Sermon on the Mount not to seek revenge nor even to resist evil, and that seems to be good advice, morally superior to the Exodus law, even if Jesus' position is much harder for us to perform in our daily lives. From such comparisons, we form an impression of Old Testament law as harsh and unyielding, as punitive and painful in the extreme.

Though Old Testament law could certainly be harsh, one must examine it in its ancient context. These Exodus laws provide limits to vengeful response that were not consistently present in other ancient people's laws. In other nations, it might be the case that a rich person killing a poor person would receive no punishment, but a poor person striking or injuring a rich person would be executed. The Old Testament laws strive to equalize these sorts of gross disparities.

Yet, from our perspective, the Old Testament laws fall far short of structuring a fair and equal society. Consider this example: if a slaveowner (already unfairness!) kills a slave, the slaveowner should be punished. The punishment would not equal the offense; slaveowners are given benefits under the law not given to their slaves. But if the slaveowner strikes the slave and the slaves dies a few days later from the injuries suffered, then there is no punishment for the slaveowner. Why? There is no punishment because the slave was merely property, and the owner can do with his property as he sees fit (Exodus 21:20–21). Slaves do not have the fullness of human rights accorded to slaveowners.

But another law perhaps would lead to a different evaluation. If a slaveowner strikes a slave, causing that slave, whether male or female, to lose an eye or a tooth, then the slaveowner must let the slave go free. The owner loses one slave, and the slave loses a tooth or an eye. It's hard for us to judge if that is fair or not, but at least it comes closer to the fairness that we would like to see, except for the presence of slavery as an accepted institution in the first place. The effect of the law, however, would be to

---

[1] David Root, Professor of New Testament at Northwest Christian College, Eugene, Oregon, often comments that the law of Exodus 21:24, if applied rigorously, would produce a lot of blind, toothless people—and such is certainly not God's intention.

discourage slaveowners from mistreating their slaves, because these owners would risk the loss of their investment if they injured their slaves. Thus this law works to protect slaves from abuse, and as such it would have been a helpful and maybe even enlightened law in its time. The fact that it seems barbarous to us reflects how far we have come toward establishing equal rights, even though we still fall far short of the mark of equality and fairness in social relations.

Though there are numerous differences in detail, ancient Israelite law usually treated women as slaves, at least in one sense. With both slaves and women, a similar ethical logic shaped the laws. Both were property of some man, and any damage to a slave or a woman would require compensation to the man who owned that slave or woman. Likewise, the same logic applied to land issues and matters of objects or animals. Though punishments would differ, the murder of a man's ox and the murder of a man's wife or daughter were both considered affronts to the man, who should then be compensated for *his* loss. The feelings of the slave, the ox, or the woman were rarely taken into consideration. In the applications of such laws, the degradation of women becomes quite obvious.

Three situations in the legal codes shape certain narratives in the book of Genesis regarding the roles and status of women. These laws govern marriage, childbearing, and rape. Whereas the laws show us the theoretical means by which Israelites would deal with these situations, the narratives show us in more human terms the ways that these events combined with the law to affect women's lives.

Fighting Over Jacob

Jacob and Laban

Jacob's life is a story of his struggle for control.[2] He begins to struggle with his brother, Esau, in Rebekah's womb (Genesis 25:24–26), and their fighting and trickery for preeminence never stops throughout their lives (Genesis 27:41–45; 32:3–21). Jacob struggles with Esau for the birthright (Genesis 25:29–34), and

---

[2]See Nelly Furman, "His Story Versus Her Story: Male Genealogy and Female Strategy in the Jacob Cycle," *Semeia* 46 (1989): pp. 141–149. Cp. Susan Niditch, *Underdogs and Tricksters: A Prelude to Biblical Folklore,* New Voices in Biblical Studies (San Francisco: Harper and Row, 1987).

Jacob struggles with his father, Isaac, for the blessing and inheritance (Genesis 27:1–29). Jacob even struggles with God, and goes away a winner (Genesis 32:22–32).[3] Jacob struggles for control, and mostly he struggles for control of *things*. He strives to achieve inheritance so that he can possess more things. Even in his struggle with God, he seeks a thing: a new name. Jacob sees life in terms of the things around him that he can possess. This outlook makes him a wealthy man by the end of his life, but it limits his ability to deal with people. He tends to see even relatives and spouses as objects to be possessed or to manipulate so that he can increase his belongings.

Jacob is a trickster. He wins by deceiving. He tricked his brother out of his birthright and he tricked his father out of a blessing. But then the situation turns ugly, and he does what most tricksters finally end up doing—he leaves town quickly with no forwarding address. His mother knows where he has gone, but she'll never tell, since it would endanger his life. He flees to his uncle's house, to Laban, Rebekah's brother. Once there, we find out something that really shouldn't surprise us: trickery runs in the family.

Laban is also a controller and struggler, and a trickster as well. Laban is a wealthy man who intends to stay that way, and his scruples about methods for attaining and maintaining wealth might leave a little to be desired. Jacob met his match in Uncle Laban. Together, they spent a decade and a half tricking each other over the control of four women: Leah and Rachel, along with their servants Bilhah and Zilpah. In the end, Jacob wins, but someone pays the price. It takes little imagination to guess who pays.

The story began innocently enough, however. Jacob arrived in Laban's pasture, and immediately he met his winsome cousin, Rachel. It was love at first sight, and Jacob's response was predictable: he simply must have her. Possession was much more than nine tenths of Jacob's thoughts about anything, and it

---

[3]In this, Jacob provides a contrast to his grandfather, Abraham, who never struggled enough with God. When Jacob receives a new name from God, it is Israel, meaning, "he struggles with God." This name is perhaps related to that of Jacob's grandmother, Sarah, which may mean "she struggles." Still, the text of Genesis produces a vague sense that Jacob, in his struggling, takes a virtue too far. Jacob's new name, Israel, is not too different from his former name, which means "he grasps," perhaps with some negative connotations.

was all the more so with Rachel. Jacob's reaction was the natural one for him: he struck a deal with Laban. Jacob would work seven years, and for that his wages would be Rachel (plus room and board for seven years, we presume). Laban agreed instantly—he must have loved the thought of such cheap labor. For these two possessive tricksters, a deal was a deal, and the payment for labor could be cash or a woman. To them, it seemed one and the same.

This reflects a notion of the Israelite law. Marriages involved money; they were a transaction of goods. An object (a woman)was transferred from one party (her father) to another party (the husband-to-be) in exchange for a price.[4] In this case, the price was set at seven years of Jacob's employment. Rachel had no say in the matter; she was merely property bought and sold.

Jacob thought that he had the better deal here, but he soon learned that he was in the company of a better trickster than he, a true master. At the appointed time, Laban delivered the wrong daughter, and Jacob married Leah instead of Rachel. Jacob was stuck, and Laban awaited the opportunity for the crowning victory. Jacob still wanted Rachel, and Laban knew that he had what Jacob wanted. Laban, the master trickster, offered a new deal, double or nothing—another seven years for another daughter.

Rachel suffered the pain of knowing that she was merely a pawn in her father's attempts to gain wealth and power. Her marriage was at a price that would benefit him, and she had no control over her own life. In fact, the control of her life was the centerpiece of a struggle between two tricksters. But at least she knew that Jacob honestly loved her. Leah, on the other hand, knew the price of her marriage and knew one more thing—her husband didn't think that she had been worth the price. On the day after her wedding, her husband clamored to her father and mortgaged the next seven years of his life (and Leah's life, too) to buy another bride. He didn't like the model, and as soon as he drove it off the lot he started thinking about replacing it; but Jacob thought such things about *women,* about the living human who was now his own wife. To him, they were only objects, property to be negotiated.[5]

---

[4]For a discussion of bride prices and their effect on this story, see Sharon Pace Jeansonne, *The Women of Genesis: From Sarah to Potiphar's Wife* (Minneapolis: Fortress Press, 1990), pp. 72–73.

[5]The law of Leviticus 18:18 forbids sexual relations with two sisters, but this Genesis story shows no recognition of this supposedly later law.

Children at Any Cost

Jacob, Leah, and Rachel formed a family consisting of one cousin and two sisters, one nephew and two daughters married but still living at home, one husband and two wives, one loving relationship and one hateful one. With beginnings like this, it comes as no surprise that this cozy family had problems from the start. Jacob's mindset infected the women. He thought of them as property, and they thought of themselves in much the same way. He struggled to increase the value of his holdings, and Leah and Rachel struggled to increase their worth to their owner. When women are commodities and their value is measured in productivity, then they enter into struggles to achieve.

Leah and Rachel struggled over children. Each wanted to produce the precious sons that would buy them favor with Jacob. Leah's fertility was impressive, and with each son, she thought that maybe this one would buy Jacob's love (Genesis 29:31–35). But even after four sons, nothing could buy Jacob's heart. He still showed no loyalty to her, no affection. Human values do not arise from these sorts of economic transactions, no matter how well they work.

Jacob and Laban had treated Leah and Rachel like property; these women treated themselves like factories, and they struggled to deliver the product that could be bartered for what they wanted. All they desired was their husband's love and acceptance, but that turned out to be the one thing he could never really give, especially to mere objects.

Rachel's desperation to match her sister's production turned into rage, and Jacob responded in kind (Genesis 30:1–2). But then Rachel had an idea. She had been studying family history, it seems, and she had finally run across the chapter of the genealogy wherein Sarah provided her maid Hagar to Abraham for purposes of childbearing. Unfortunately, it appears that Rachel never read the rest of the story, to see where it would end. Immediately, Rachel rushed to Jacob and offered him the use of her maid, Bilhah. He was angry with her, but he accepted the offer, since it was obvious to him that there could be gain here, measured in children. Soon, Jacob had two more sons, counted in Rachel's favor though born to the maid Bilhah.

Leah did not fail to notice that her sister was gaining on her in production, even if through circumspect means, and so she raised the stakes. If Rachel could play games with maids, so could Leah. So Leah provided her maid, Zilpah. Through Zilpah,

Leah matches Rachel's two sons through Bilhah. Once again, Leah was in the lead in terms of numbers, but still it was not enough to buy Jacob's heart, even after six sons (four of them natural!) to Rachel's measly two. Leah had even produced a daughter, to add to it all. Though daughters were not worth as much in this maniacal numerology, Rachel hadn't even done that much.

Rachel's day came at last, and she produced a son, named Joseph. Those who know the rest of the story are aware that Joseph turned out to be the most favored son, and so Rachel could claim victory in quality if not in quantity. Rachel was oblivious to this future history, however. At the birth, when it was time for naming, her comment was a plea: "Just one more!" (Genesis 30:24). Rachel eventually got her wish, but when the final son came, Rachel's birthing stool sat right next to her death bed (Genesis 35:16–20). The struggle was over, but it was hard to proclaim anyone as the winner.

In the end, Leah and Rachel both sold their dignity to achieve sons. Leah never purchased her husband's love with all of her children. Rachel had love from the beginning, but wanted exclusive rights on that love; she gambled and, at the moment of her greatest achievement that might have bought her what she wanted, she lost everything.

Paying the Ultimate Price

Jacob's trickery resulted in alienation from his father-in-law, Uncle Laban. Two wives and a dozen children seemed a bit skimpy to Jacob; after all, he had been at work a long time. It seemed that Jacob had turned out to be the winner after all, but Jacob was never content with apparent victories. Jacob then plotted his final victory, the one scheme that would set him in history forever (Genesis 30:25–43). His complex scam involved shuttling sheep and peeling almond rods, but in the end it worked, and Jacob forced Laban to pay him what seemed like the ultimate price—such a large percentage of the flocks that Jacob became magnificently wealthy. In the process, he alienated everyone around him, and he soon needed to leave town on short notice (Genesis 31:1—32:21). Jacob knew the routine; it wasn't the first time for him.

Jacob suffered for his trickery, but his compensation was wealth of flocks. He thought that he had paid a high price, so he struggled to get even. But his cost was puny in comparison to the high price that others paid. Leah lived a life of disgrace with no respect at all. Rachel died in childbirth, paying the ultimate price to give a baby boy to a man who still played boys' games.

Dinah's Journey

Starting Down the Path

A few years went by, and now the oldest of Jacob's children were full-grown adults, learning the limits of their responsibilities and possibilities in the world. Leah's daughter, Dinah, set out on a journey (Genesis 34:1). She may have wanted to see the world, or just to stretch her wings for a while. She started down the path to finding her own future, venturing outside the craziness of Jacob's family that was all she had ever known. When she started out, she didn't know where it would end. Had she foreseen the future, she might never have started in the first place.

Dinah started her story by avoiding the games that men play. She had seen enough of those games in her young life; her father played those games all the time and Dinah was not unaware of the pain that those games caused to her mother and to her recently departed aunt, Rachel. Dinah needed out from under Jacob for a while to clear her mind and to start to think about what life could offer. Would there ever be another way for women? Could another kind of life be possible, or was the best for which one could hope a life as someone else's property? She set off in search of answers. She sojourned to visit with other women, and to talk with them about their lives. Perhaps in the company of women, away from the absurdities of men like Jacob and Laban, she could understand what life was really like for women.

Dinah's journey of honest inquiry soon turned to one of danger, as one would expect for women who tried to move outside the system accepted and controlled by men. She wanted to see what life was like outside of Jacob's treatment of women as property. She found that women were degraded everywhere. Her search for a safe community of women became violated by men, and once more the men treated her as an object and vied for control of her.

Dinah and the Prince

For a single verse, Dinah was an actor, an inquirer. She wanted to discover if there was a way for women to live as people, instead of as objects. With the start of the second verse, she received an answer, and for the rest of the story, she was an object.

The story turned around when Shechem entered. Shechem was a local prince who noticed Dinah and immediately raped her. To Shechem, Dinah was an object, and as the object of the prince's desire, he could seize that object as his own. After all, there was no one around to stop him. Surprisingly, Shechem then fell in love with Dinah. We might expect true love (and there is no reason to doubt Shechem's sincerity at this point) to help the situation, but it is already too late. Things are already very bad, and from here they can only get worse.

Their Father's Sons

Shechem wanted to marry Dinah, and so he asked his father, Hamor, to make the appropriate arrangements with Dinah's family (Genesis 34:4). At first, Jacob and all of Dinah's brothers did not take kindly to this news and this outrageous proposal of marriage. Hamor, however, could not be stopped; he kept going on about the true love that Shechem felt for Dinah. Then, Hamor tried to appeal to the men's greed and lust; he promised wives for them all. Even this produced no results. Hamor pulled one more trick out of his bag, and it turned out to be the right offer for this crowd. Hamor offered Jacob and his sons some economic advantages, in the form of trading rights, if they would consent to give Dinah, their beloved sister, to Shechem, the avowed rapist. Jacob and the boys could not pass up a deal like that.

Jacob was caught speechless for just an instant, so his sons stepped forward with their hearty agreement. But they made their acceptance contingent on one matter: they would allow Dinah's marriage only after all the males in Shechem's family underwent circumcision (Genesis 34:15). Hamor and Shechem accepted the terms and shook hands with Dinah's brothers, sealing the deal. They set an enthusiastic timetable and everyone agreed to it. Then they all went their separate ways, pleased with their deal to trade Dinah for profit.

But the situation was not what it seemed. Dinah's brothers proved that they were their father's sons. Jacob had lived and gained by trickery, and now his sons devised a plot to use their religion to trick the Shechemites into weakness and death. Like father, like sons. All of them sought to prosper through treachery, and all of them failed to blink at the sight of a woman abused.

The Trap

The knife fell on every male of Shechem's family, and three days later the brothers sprung their trap. They stormed the unsuspecting, pain-wracked Shechemites and killed each one with the sword. Then they plundered their villages. In order to avenge the defiling of their sister, they defiled a whole people through genocide, rape, and pillaging. It all was just the right thing to do, they thought, to defend their property, their sister.

Property seemed to be the family's only concern. Jacob's sons gained a lot of it through their attack and plundering, including land, flocks, personal property, and probably also an opportunity to take over Hamor's trading routes and that potential for profit. They also gained women as part of their plunder. These Shechemite women now became secondary wives, married to the murderers of their husbands. Of course, no one cared about their desires; as women and as foreigners, these women were only property, without rights, even the right to an opinion. When Jacob found out what his sons had done, he was appalled, but then the readers discover his reason. He was concerned about his image, and he feared that there might be dangerous reprisals that could be quite costly. No one would want that, would they?

Apparently, none of Jacob's family ever questioned the ethics of using their faith as a ruse to cover up murder. Their holy rite of circumcision became nothing more than an excuse to weaken the enemy. Even the most important and sacred religious practices served as means to property; rituals were things to be used for their own personal benefit. This attitude could well be blasphemy, but there was no sign of second thoughts. Any means would serve in the struggle to achieve advantage over others.

The law about an eye for an eye and a tooth for a tooth came later, centuries after this episode. As far as Jacob's sons were concerned, the only law was the law of the sword, and the equation of that law was much different. A few villages for a rape seemed just about right. Besides, the Shechemites wanted to give Jacob's family some economic advantages, anyway; why not just take the ultimate advantage?

The End of the Road

What about Dinah? Did anyone in the story still care about her? It seems hard to think that they did.

As a rape victim, she became damaged property. She could have married her rapist, Shechem, but now her only possible mate was dead at the hands of her ever-loving brothers (cf. Deuteronomy 22:25–29). They consigned her to a life of solitude. Throughout all of the brothers' actions, they never asked her about what she wanted, and they never thought about how to help her. Instead, they only considered what would help their finances and their reputation.

Violence begat violence, and many people died, but Dinah's own problems as a victim were ignored. Because she was property to be bought and sold, she never spoke and never acted throughout the story, even though the tale began when she journeyed to speak with other women. She began an innocent person with vivacious curiosity and hopes for a magnificent future, but she ended the story thoroughly crushed with no hopes at all, even though her brothers had made themselves rich through the situation.

Blaming the Victims

Victimization runs rampant through these stories. Jacob and Laban take advantage of each other repeatedly; each enjoys it until it looks like the other is winning. In the thrashing of their struggles, they injure others almost without noticing. Leah and Rachel enter as victims, as pawns of men's struggles for power. Each becomes victimizer of the other in order to maintain whatever worth they have received through this evil system of treating women as property. Since each victimizes, then each is a victim from multiple sources. They attempt to gain advantage over each other, but the only result is the increase of their pain. Many interpreters blame Leah and Rachel for their rivalry. The victims receive the blame.

Dinah is the innocent victim of rape, but she becomes the catalyst for genocide. The text almost criticizes Dinah; she was the one who left the protection of home and went out on the road by herself. The law blames the victim who was raped when others were around, because she could have cried out and found help (Deuteronomy 22:23–24). In that sense, the rape is Dinah's fault, and she can even be blamed for the resulting genocide. The Shechemites receive a mass death sentence that they did not deserve, but the brothers blame it on them. They are the victims of the pillaging and murder, but it still remains their fault. When

Jacob questions (for his own selfish reasons) his sons' overreaction, they respond that they had no choice, because of Dinah's reputation. The blood of a people's destruction sullies her, as well. Again, the victim receives the blame.

Blaming the victim is an old reaction, the kind of trick of which Jacob would be proud. But blaming victims only increases the victimization. In bad marriages such as Leah, Rachel, and Jacob's, and in tragic situations such as Dinah's, blaming the victim never helps the victim, who most needs the help. Blaming the victim may be a popular attempt to control the situation, but it only makes things worse, both for the victim and for everyone else around, because it sends the situation spiraling out of anyone's control.

Chapter 6

Women Who
Take Charge

As seen in the last chapter, many women within ancient Israel were bought and sold without any consideration of their own desires. Women were treated as property by law and by custom. They had very little control over their own lives. However, there were numerous exceptions. Many women took control of their own lives and shaped their own destinies. Though these cases were rare and probably considered countercultural or at least risqué, there were opportunities for at least some women to break out of the typical expectations and find ways to control their own situations. Some of the women in ancient Israel did take charge of their own lives.

Any woman from those times who did take charge of her own life probably began by resisting the control of the men in her life. Throughout the culture, men worked to control women and to limit their options to the accepted roles of childbearing. To find any other path through life, women first had to resist the ways that men tried to control them. In the case of Dinah, she attempted to take charge of her own life by leaving home to associate with other women, but she failed because she could not defend herself against the force of Shechem. But other women were able to resist the controls of men and thus they could create a space around themselves in which they could begin to exercise their own control.

Of course, this path is not without its own problems. Any choice in life has its own pitfalls, and riskier paths tend to have more potential for trouble. One inherent danger is that resisting control and taking charge of one's own life involves using control. When I am a victim of someone else's controlling power, I may consider that use of power to be wrong and manipulative, but the only solution often is to use control myself, running the risk of becoming as manipulative as others. Control is a dangerous thing; it can very easily become addictive power that hurts others and limits the opportunities for life as much as taking charge can enhance those possibilities.

This is undoubtedly true, and yet this line of thinking itself has been used frequently to control women. Our own terminology can betray us. Our culture calls controlling men assertive, take-charge guys who know what they want and do what it takes to get it. But our culture calls women with the same traits bitches who will scratch out the eyes of others. Control is admirable in men, but our culture still prefers women who are soft, docile, and accepting of the men who are in control.

Because of these strong cultural biases, we must be careful how we evaluate strong women in the Old Testament stories. We must be sure to affirm their assertiveness for the positive thing that it is. Yet we must also remember the dangers of power and control. Women can damage others and even themselves with abuses of power just as men can. All persons, both women and men, must walk a fine line between taking charge of one's life and manipulating others. But for women this fine line may become so small that it just disappears, because of the ways that men, consciously or not, try to control them. Perhaps it will take a great deal of power for any woman to resist the control of men and to take charge of her own life. Thus any use of power must be seen in its larger context. What is at stake? Is it worth the price of power? Autonomy is greatly to be valued, yet at times the costs may be too high. Still, for women, autonomy requires empowerment, or at least self-empowerment, and that may only come at a great price that we must be willing to pay.

Where do we strike the balance between empowerment for authentic autonomy and abuse of power for manipulative damage? The question is most difficult. This chapter offers two examples from the end of the book of Genesis, two stories in which women take charge in attempts to empower their own lives. We should ask whether they cross the line from autonomy to abuse. The texts will provide us with all the clues we need to find the answers, and the answers may surprise us.

Seduction in Egypt

The first of these stories occurs in Genesis 39, when an Egyptian official's wife attempts to seduce Jacob's son, Joseph. At the time, Joseph belonged to the official; he was an Egyptian slave. The wife tries to take charge of her life and also Joseph's situation, playing on her position of power as an Egyptian. But we need some background first.

Joseph's Vulnerability

Joseph was Jacob's second youngest son, the first child by Rachel, and so Joseph enjoyed a special, privileged position within the family. Though he was eleventh in the rank of the sons, he was the eldest son of the favorite wife. This gave him influence, but he was still younger and littler than his ten big brothers, who really did not want to bother with a young upstart like Joseph.

Then the. dreams started. Joseph kept dreaming that he would be the superior of the brothers and that he would overcome his youth to gain power. When that happened, he dreamed, his brothers would fall down and honor him (Genesis 37:1–11). Of course, the dreams themselves were hardly Joseph's fault. How could he help it? But he made the situation worse. He told his brothers about the dreams. "Guess what, big brother? Someday you'll fall to the ground and kiss my feet!" Understandably, this made the brothers very upset. These brothers never took offenses lightly, as we saw when they reacted to their sister's rape through profitable genocide. Joseph was only a naive child, but he had already set himself up for a fall.

One day, the ten older brothers were away working in the fields. Joseph, meanwhile, had stayed home, to play with his dad. He was too young to work, but probably his brothers didn't see things that way. Then Jacob sent Joseph into the fields to check up on his brothers and report back to his father (Genesis 37:12–18). But his brothers saw him coming, and they had a chance to think about what they could do. They plotted to kill him. They would get rid of that little troublemaker once and for all. Reuben, the eldest son, suggested that this was a bit harsh. After all, they were all brothers, or half-brothers, in this case. Reuben's idea was to throw Joseph in a pit, so that the brothers' hands would not be covered with blood. Let him die of starvation there. The story tells us that Reuben intended to go back to the pit and rescue Joseph (Genesis 37:21–22). Reuben didn't want to kill his baby brother, just to frighten him thoroughly. It just might do him some good. So the brothers seized Joseph, stripped him naked, and tossed him into a pit.

As the brothers sat around dinner that night, Judah had another idea. Along came a caravan of Ishmaelites, these brothers' second cousins. They were traders, wandering through the desert buying and selling to make their living. Perhaps they would be interested in buying Joseph as a slave. That solved both problems—how to get rid of Joseph and how to escape bloodguilt for killing him—and had an added benefit, since the brothers would be paid for this slave. These brothers could never pass up a good incentive like that, and so they sold Joseph to the slave-traders. The ten brothers split twenty shekels' profit from the deal to boot.

Reuben thought up the cover-up of the sale. They still had Joseph's fancy coat, so they slaughtered a goat and soaked the coat in the goat's blood, then took the robe to Jacob. Jacob recognized it and felt certain that Joseph had been killed by wild beasts. None of the brothers bothered to tell Jacob anything different.

The point of this story seems clear: the brothers controlled Joseph. To them, he was nothing more than a nuisance, a potential slave, and a quick profit. As brother, Joseph had been vulnerable, and now as a slave that vulnerability would only become worse. He could be controlled by anyone, and eventually he was passed from one owner to another, with some stays in jail in between. He had no capacity to control his own life, except that the dreams continued. One day, those dreams would save him, but that part of the story was still far away. For the time being, Joseph was vulnerable to others' control.

Potiphar's Wife

The Ishmaelite traders took the victim Joseph to Egypt and sold him there to the highest bidder. Joseph, the favorite son of a very wealthy man, was bought and sold like a common slave, even like a woman. Though Joseph was a slave, life was not too harsh with him yet. Potiphar bought Joseph, and Potiphar was a high-ranking Egyptian official. He gave Joseph the run of his house, and made him the manager of all Potiphar's property and personal business. This was a very high position for a slave, and Joseph proved capable of the tasks and their large responsibility.

No matter how high he rose, however, Joseph was still a slave, and there was a huge gulf between the most important slave and least important slaveowner.

It was in this position as manager of household affairs for Potiphar that Joseph came to the notice of Potiphar's wife, whom the story never named. As the wife of such a high-ranking official within the Egyptian court bureaucracy, Potiphar's wife was accustomed to having things her way. She existed in a strange contradiction of statuses. Because of her husband, she was extremely powerful. But because she was a woman, her rights to own property or to make decisions were greatly limited. What ability did she truly have to control her own life, to take what she wanted? Potiphar's wife decided that what she wanted was Joseph, and she set out to have him as her lover.

The woman approached Joseph and, in no uncertain terms, requested sex from him (Genesis 39:7). He refused; she continued. One day, he veered a bit too close, and she seized him by the hem of his robe. She pulled it off of him, and he ran away from her, stark naked. Frustrated by her seeming inability to exercise any control that would gain her what she wanted, she settled for a control that would damage. She called to her other servants and to her husband, and she falsely accused the boy Joseph of attempting rape. "Look," she said, "he ran away when I shouted and here's his cloak to prove it. See how bravely I resisted him!"

The lies are thick. Joseph did not disrobe willingly; he lost his cloak to the seizure of others, now for the second time with equally bad results for him. There had been no attempted rape on Joseph's part, though it was now inevitable that he would be blamed for it and would suffer the punishment for the uncommitted crime.

But the greatest lies were those that Potiphar's wife told herself. She tried to convince herself that negative power would be as satisfying as positive power, but Joseph's punishment and removal would do nothing to help her feel better. She tried to tell herself and others that she had resisted Joseph's attempts to control her, but quite the opposite was true. In her attempts to take charge of her own life, she tried to manipulate Joseph by using her considerable power over him as slave, but she cannot coerce him, even after repeated vain attempts. The first step to self-determination is resisting others' control. Potiphar's wife did not resist Joseph; he resisted her, and showed the truly successful control, even though he lost control of his own fate in the process.

Perhaps worst of all, Potiphar's wife thought that she had power to control her own life. But in the end, Joseph had the power to resist, and Potiphar had the power to send Joseph away. Potiphar's wife ended the story with absolutely no control at all. Once Potiphar entered the scene, he took all power and control upon himself. Once more, male control eclipsed women's power to self-determination.

Another Message

Another issue enters the text. We would expect that Joseph refused because of the great danger that his master, Potiphar, would pose if Joseph accepted the woman's invitation. But Joseph himself offered another reason; he raised the rhetorical stakes by claiming that the act would anger God (Genesis 39:9). Joseph brought God and divine legitimation into his use of power, asserting that he must follow a higher authority than a prominent Egyptian official who happened to own him. But this creates a further contrast within the story. Obviously, male power defeated female power, and male slave-owner power defeated male slave power, but male *piety* also defeated female power. This is a dangerous notion.

Certainly, there is a positive role played by Potiphar's wife in this story. She moves the narrative along. Potiphar's house is not the right place for Joseph, and this conflict with Potiphar's wife drives him out of that house and, eventually, into a place where he can fulfill his God-given goal. Of course, this was not the intention of Potiphar's wife, but she functions as a key to the eventual salvation of Israel through Joseph.[1] Had she never made her move on Joseph, Joseph would never have moved out of Potiphar's care. Though Joseph would not have seen the incident as positive, it did work out well in the end.

In the flow of the whole story of Joseph's life (Genesis 37—50), Potiphar's wife plays the role of helper, albeit a very inadvertent helper whose "help" in moving along the narrative is not appreciated by any of the other characters at that point in the tale. Perhaps this provides the best commentary on women's

---

[1]Susan Tower Hollis, "The Woman in Ancient Examples of the Potiphar's Wife Motif, K2111," in *Gender and Difference in Ancient Israel*, ed. Peggy L. Day (Minneapolis: Fortress Press, 1989), pp. 28–42.

power in this story. Male piety opposes women's power even when women work to further God's purpose, and male power crushes women's power even though the men do not understand or appreciate women.

Tamar's Trials

For the young woman Tamar, life itself was a series of trials and difficulties, and the end nearly came at a legal trial that put her very life on the line because of the way she had used power to set her own course in life. But at that final trial, at the last minute, she received the approval for her power, and she became known as righteous for her own acts of self-determination.

The History of Jacob's Family

The children of Jacob the trickster were a somewhat surly bunch. Though they grew up to be great ancestors of the twelve tribes of Israel, according to the retellings of the history their early experiences were rather checkered. Dinah's rape resulted in the brothers' genocide of the Shechemites. Reuben made a mark for himself by fathering children with his own father's concubine, Bilhah. Joseph, the young dreamer, was sold into slavery by his brothers. Now the story turns for a chapter toward Judah.

Judah decided to move away from his brothers, to get a little space of his own. He settled down and married a Canaanite woman, and soon thereafter he had three sons, Er, Onan, and Shelah. When the time came, Judah bought a wife for his oldest son, Er. Her name was Tamar (Genesis 38:1–6).

Tamar and Her Husbands

Er and Tamar did all the things that newlyweds do, settling down for a long life together. But God had other plans. Er was an evil man, and God decided that Er did not deserve to live, and so God struck Er dead. Tamar the newlywed became Tamar the young widow. Fortunately, the law had a remedy for this situation. Tamar's problem was that she had neither husband nor son to support her, and this resulted in Tamar's financial marginality. The law's solution was that Tamar would then marry the next oldest son. Judah did the right thing by Tamar, and she and Onan were soon married.

This reaction, spurred by the law, solved Tamar's problem, but Onan did not much care for it. After all, any sons of that union would be counted as Er's sons; they would inherit Er's share of Judah's sizable estate and they would, in years to come, care for Tamar as their mother, not for Onan and any other wives he might have by then. Judah had always been quick to observe where the profit was, and his son took after him. Onan saw that there was no profit in providing Tamar with children, and so Onan made sure that Tamar did not get pregnant. Practicing *coitus interruptus,* Onan enjoyed sexual relations with Tamar without allowing her the benefit of producing children that could care for her (Genesis 38:9). God observed Onan's selfishness, and so God killed him. Judah had now lost two sons and Tamar was a widow for the second time.

Tamar remained childless through two marriages, brief though they seem to have been, yet she was not barren. The childlessness was in no way her fault. In fact, this story reverses the curse of barrenness. Usually, this ancient society assumed that childlessness was the fault of the woman, and so it was no great tragedy if lack of children meant that she had no means for financial support in her later years. The barrenness in early life and the impoverishment in later life corresponded, just as if God had planned it that way, providing a reason for suffering. But here it is right to blame Tamar's childlessness on her husbands, and so they experienced the loss of life that should match barrenness. No matter how appropriate the situation, however, Tamar was still left in an extremely tenuous condition. Once more, she was the childless widow.

The law had once more been activated, and Judah was obligated to marry his youngest son, Shelah, to Tamar. But he resisted the power of law, because he was afraid that he would lose this third son to the death that apparently plagued all Tamar's mates (Genesis 38:11). Judah and Tamar became involved in a contest of wills. Judah had the needed commodity (a son) and Tamar had the law on her side. But fathers need sons, too. Shelah was the last relative with direct responsibility to care for Judah in his old age, and he was scared to think of losing that guarantee of support, if Shelah should die in his marriage to Tamar. Judah knew that Tamar now had no means of support, but he was unwilling to share Shelah and risk his own guarantee just to let her have a way to live.[2] Both Judah and Tamar quested

---

[2] It may also be true that Judah's greed disadvantaged Shelah as well by forbidding the marriage.

after financial security, and Judah controlled it in ways that maximized his chances while minimizing her possibilities to zero. For these reasons, Judah refused the marriage, but of course he could not say so publicly. Instead, he postponed it indefinitely.

Tamar left Judah's household and returned to her father's household, where she was allowed to live in poverty as an outcast. At least there she could eat and work, even though she had lost all respect and dignity. She could not marry anyone else, because she was legally bound to Judah's family and to the eldest unmarried male. Judah was cheating according to the law by withholding Shelah from her, but there was nothing she could do. Women did not have the power to force a man's hand on an issue such as this. Over the years, as she grew older, her desperation grew, but Judah was untouchable in his violation of both law and decency.

A Plan

Then Judah's wife died, and when Tamar heard of it, she formed a plan. She knew that Judah would not deprive himself of sex for long, and the shearing season was about to approach. Shearing season had a reputation for sexual activity that seems to have been well deserved.[3] With that bit of information, Tamar knew exactly what she would do.

Tamar dressed herself as a prostitute, covered with a veil, and went to stand alongside the road where Judah would pass. She was right; Judah propositioned her as soon as he saw her. She set a reasonable price, one goat, but she knew that Judah would not have a spare goat with him at the moment. Instead, she accepted Judah's promise of future payment, and she took his signet ring, his cord, and his staff as an I.O.U. Then they both went on their ways, and Tamar returned to her widow's garments. Judah was never the wiser about what happened, though he may have wondered why he could not find the woman with his ring, cord, and staff to trade the goat for them.

A few months passed, and then Tamar sprung the trap.

The Trial

Tamar leaked the news of her pregnancy, and the gossip soon reached Judah. It couldn't have made Judah happier, be-

---

[3]In our culture, one thinks of the tittering comments made about winter cold snaps and the children born nine months later.

cause now he had the chance to finish this problem once and for all. Since she had clearly been unfaithful and had violated her widowhood, she had lost all of her rights to Judah's precious Shelah. Furthermore, Judah now had just cause to have her killed, so that she could never try to take anything from Judah's family ever again. He thought of her as a gold digger, and he would soon be rid of her. Judah sent out the word to have Tamar burned at the stake in punishment for her unfaithfulness. The trial was over; Judah served as prosecutor, judge, and jury. Tamar would die.

At the last minute, Tamar sent word to Judah. A messenger rushed to Judah with news that would be sure to make Judah happy, he thought: "The father of Tamar's child is the owner of these!" The messenger handed a ring, a cord, and a staff to Judah, positive that Judah would be pleased to know the truth of the matter. Perhaps it was another of Judah's enemies who could now be sentenced to death as well. If nothing else, the father of the child might have heard from Tamar about Judah's misdealings with her, and such rumors could be firmly silenced at once.

Judah looked at the objects, and the whole situation changed instantly. He knew that he had been wrong. The messenger stood waiting for instructions, but Judah offered a strange command: "Don't kill Tamar."

Tamar emerged victorious. Her power and her deceit proved stronger than Judah's in the end. She won the chance to live, and she won a husband—old rich Judah himself. She also had the offspring needed to secure her future, and in six months, she was the mother of twin boys, Perez and Zerah.[4] Her power succeeded. She took charge of her own future and she won.

True Righteousness

Tamar won more than the sons; she won the respect of men, including the man whom she tricked and forced. Judah's last words in this story are much more than striking; they are absolutely amazing considering what has just happened: "She is more righteous than I am" (Genesis 38:26). Tamar the trickster, Tamar the spurned, Tamar the prostitute, Tamar the incestuous is Tamar

---

[4]This inclusion of a righteous woman with great audacity made such an impact on people's minds that Tamar appears in the genealogy of Jesus in Matthew 1:3. See Bernard Brandon Scott, "The Birth of the Reader," *Semeia* 52 (1990): 83–102.

the righteous. Her use of female power was exceptionally strong, strong enough to violate several of Israel's laws, but it made her righteous. She assaulted common decency and common sense, but it made her righteous. She sought what she needed to survive and stopped at absolutely nothing to achieve it. That is righteousness personified. She risked her own life to attain it, but that only adds to the purity of her actions. Despite actions that could rightly be called sin, she is righteous.

Tamar's case is not a comparison of male piety against female power. Female power is exalted, not denied. Piety does not contradict power, but the use of power for the right ends transcends the bonds of piety or legality. Female righteousness, in violation of all sense of order, defeated the male power and control that threatened to snuff out Tamar's possibilities for life.

Perhaps that is the key here. Tamar was willing to do anything to stay alive and to prosper. Any actions taken in that direction, despite their legality, were righteous acts because they moved in the direction of life. Her choice to pay any price only underscored and verified her intentions, as did her originality in forming a plan of action.

By Tamar's example, women legitimately take any means necessary to ensure their own survival and prosperity. Since men work so hard to limit women in the ancient world as well as in this one, women must take extraordinary means to achieve their survival. Even if the actions break the law as Tamar's did, they are still righteous acts because they work for life. Female power attacking male control is appropriate and righteous. Subservience is no answer; breaking the system to insist on justice at any cost is the way God desires and respects.

Chapter 7

Women
Who Proclaim
the Faith

What should women say about their faith?

We still wrestle with this question, more than three thousand years after the two stories in this chapter. We don't have an answer upon which all people of faith can agree. In fact, we aren't even close. Questions tear churches apart. Can women be ordained? Can women teach about the faith? Can women serve communion? Can women perform baptisms? Can women preach?

Phrasing the questions in this way conceals the point. Of course women *can* do these and many other acts of faith; women have been doing them for millennia. A more accurate question is: Will men *allow* women to proclaim their faith? That question remains unanswered on the large scale. Some denominations *allow* ordination of women; others prevent it. Some *allow* active, public, respected roles for women laity; others prevent it. Regardless of these structural concerns, women continue to have faith and continue to express and proclaim that faith. The difference is that some women receive encouragement and support for their believing and proclaiming, while other women are encouraged to keep quiet and let men do the talking about faith. Thus, some of women's proclamation is official and some is clandestine.

In the Old Testament, women proclaim their faith. Despite the strong desires of men to keep women in silence, women's voices break through the barriers. Admittedly, these women's proclamations are few and far between; the dominant male culture succeeded in stifling most of the women, at least in the recorded written sources. But some speech still comes through. Among the prophets, we find Huldah (2 Kings 22:14–20). When, in the days of King Josiah, priests found an ancient and sacred book hidden away in the temple, the chief priest Hilkiah sought out the prophet Huldah for an explanation. Huldah was able to understand the book and to discuss its ramifications with the priests, and they carried her message back to the king. This woman understood the deep matters of faith and proclaimed them in ways that made even chief priests and kings take notice.

There are a few women such as Huldah who boldly proclaim their faith, but they are very few. Perhaps there were women among the authors of the psalms, but this cannot be known. Certainly, many of the Old Testament stories were originally transmitted orally, passed down from mother to daughter through the generations until they became part of the official, written record, but recovering these oral stories in their first form is exceedingly difficult. Though women must have been involved with the stories and songs of ancient Israel's faith, most traces of their contributions have been erased through the years of male domination.

Throughout the past three thousand years and more, there has been a strong tendency for men to oppose women's proclamation of the faith and women's involvement in the official capacities of the religious community's works. Men often attempt to control and limit women's roles, and the machinery of the bureaucracies, whether official or informal, is right at hand to enforce such restrictive desires. Despite this discouragement and obstruction, women continue to come forward to proclaim their faith in vibrant, effective ways. In recent decades, churches and other religious communities have made great strides toward a fuller inclusion of women in proclamation and ministry, though the opposition is still strong, as it was once for Miriam.

Miriam's Proclamation

Origins

Miriam first appears as a nameless child in Exodus 2. Her appearance in that chapter is fleeting and almost supernatural. She enters and exits with hardly anyone noticing her, except for one key line of dialogue. It is almost as if God sent an angel, a supernatural creature, to mold history with a short series of words and then to disappear, unnoticed. Only when Miriam appears in the story later do we realize where her origins were.

A Levite man and a Levite woman married and had children while they were living with all the Hebrew people, Jacob's descendants, in Egypt. Originally invited as guests of the Pharaoh, times had changed and now the Hebrews were slaves in that land. The Egyptian government began to fear a population explosion by this ethnic minority, and so they developed a policy of birthrate reduction (which was quite antithetic to the early Israelite experience, when they had to maximize the population in as short a time as possible). Every female Hebrew baby would be allowed to live, but all male Hebrew babies would be cast into the river to drown.

With this legislation in place, it was a dangerous time to bear children. The Levite couple first had a daughter, who would grow to be Miriam. But the second child was a boy. The couple hid the child for a few months, hoping that the law would change, but soon they could no longer pretend. The boy's mother placed him on a small raft and cast him down the Nile. The boy's older sister stood at a distance, waiting to see what would transpire.

Then the raft floated down to the place where Pharaoh's daughter happened to be bathing, and Pharaoh's daughter noticed the child. Miriam wandered through, and delivered her one sentence of dialogue: she offered to find a Hebrew wet-nurse for this Hebrew child, so that Pharaoh's daughter could raise him as her own. Then Miriam sought her mother to be that wet-nurse. Mother and son were reunited. The story gives the reader an ironic wink over the shoulder of Pharaoh's daughter, who may be an unknowing participant in this affair or who may be a co-conspirator with the other women. Miriam brought about this salvation of the child through her quiet observation and her one timely sentence of speech. But few single lines in the whole Bible have changed the flow of the narrative as much as Miriam's soft suggestion that saved a baby boy and eventually gave the Hebrew people their savior, Moses.

The tradition has paid much less attention to Miriam than to her two younger brothers, Moses and Aaron. In this first scene, Miriam does not even have a name. In many of the most memorable scenes of Moses and Aaron's work, Miriam does not even appear. Yet it seems that she accompanied them throughout all of their tasks, assisting as needed. She was the quiet companion, the one who watched from a distance and did the one right thing to change the situation when it began to go wrong. Without Miriam, there would not have been a Moses to confront Pharaoh and to lead the Hebrew people out of Egypt. Miriam is Moses' origin. This act of faith by a pious woman in her youth must not go unnoticed or unaccepted in our traditions.

A Ministry of Celebration

Miriam next enters the story at the high point of the Exodus event itself. The narrative notices her again as soon as the people have miraculously crossed over the Red Sea. Moses then sang a wonderful song of praise to God who had delivered the Israelites (Exodus 15:1–18). Miriam must have been standing around Moses the whole time, but the narrative never mentions her. Just as at the time of Moses' river journey, Miriam stands and watches, waiting for the right moment to act with just the right words.

With the women of Israel, she sings and dances the song of faith after the whole people cross the Red Sea. She teaches them to sing. Miriam understands praise, the language of faith, even better than Moses does. Moses' song is hardly a hymn; it is more of a sermon. It teaches about the event. Miriam's song is joyful; it lives in the middle of the event and celebrates it as it happens, when the emotions are freshest and clearest. Miriam also understands that songs are best when sung *together*. Moses' song is a solo, designed for a congregation to sit in silence and listen to the one voice in all of its mastery and finery. Miriam's song is a chorus; *everybody sings.* Not only do they sing, but they take up tambourines to keep the rhythm and enhance the sense of celebration. With this joyful chorus in their throats and tambourines bouncing in their hands, the women join Miriam and dance together to celebrate God's wonderful goodness. This is true praise. Praise should be corporate; there should be many voices, not just one. Praise should be fun and joyful, capable of sustaining a tune and a beat. Praise should be contagious. Praise should involve the whole body, integrating the complete self in worship of God. Miriam understands praise and leads all the women in this magnificent celebration and experience of God.

It is quite possible that Miriam's song was the original one. Usually, songs start out short and then grow in length as more verses are added. Clearly, Miriam's song contains the essential element. If this is right, then Miriam's song was a more spontaneous expression of joy and faith, and Moses' song was a more reflective summary of the whole event. If this is the case, then though Moses receives the credit for that song, Miriam and her sisters in the faith sing first. Miriam feels the emotion of the moment and leads other women in expressing their deepest joy at salvation. She knows praise and brings the women to their feet to shout praise, to share their joy with the whole community.

Of course, even if Miriam's praise was first, it takes second place in the tradition's presentation. Moses' song comes first and takes the most space; it's clearly the most polished and complete of the two songs. But that represents well one of the problems of modern notions of leadership. We often think that the best leadership is the most polished piece. The best sermon, for instance, is the one with each phrase well-rounded. We devalue spontaneity in our mainline, polished, churches' ministries. Many of our churches have moved so far away from emotion and from the involvement of the whole body and soul that we shy away from the vibrant ministry provided by Miriam and her sisters today.

Sharing Leadership

Miriam appears in Moses' story one more time. Again, the issue is the sharing of leadership. How will this community's three ministers, Moses, Aaron, and Miriam, cooperate in the service of God? Aaron and Miriam both complain that Moses is usurping the roles that rightfully belong to others. Miriam and Aaron argue for a shared ministry; Moses contends for control. Moses' siblings ask, "Has Yahweh only spoken through Moses? Hasn't God also spoken through us?" (Numbers 12:2). Miriam and Aaron never ask for sole authority or for higher power, but only for an opportunity to share their voices, which they feel also represent Yahweh's voice in the same way that Moses' speech does.

Yahweh made a statement of support, and the tradition interpreted it as support for Moses (Numbers 12:6–8). Yahweh claimed that Moses had a unique relationship with God, so that Moses had special knowledge about God that others did not have. If Moses possessed some privileged relationship with God, then it may well be proper to side with Moses in this dispute. His siblings perhaps should not have questioned his authority.

Yahweh's words, however, can be taken in the opposite direction. Yahweh first argues that prophets do have special knowledge of God, based on their particularly close relationship with God (Numbers 12:6). Even though this knowledge is not as great as Moses', it is still a valid basis for ministry. Miriam has already been identified as a prophet (Exodus 15:20), and so she qualifies as one with this kind of potential for ministry. Had she asked to be greater than Moses, or even equal to Moses, she would have been in the wrong. But her remark at the beginning is of a much milder character, "Hasn't God also spoken through me?" Yahweh's answer in the oracle is clear: yes, God also speaks through Miriam, the prophet.

Miriam does not ask to take over the ministry and kick her little brother out of the picture. All she asks is to share her voice with the people, but this request is roundly refused, despite God's statement that Miriam as prophet does have important things to say within the total ministry. God's punishment is swift; Miriam is covered with leprosy. Women who presume to contribute their voice deserve punishment, or so the story seems to state.

Interestingly, Aaron had made the same exact complaint as Miriam did at the start, yet he receives no such punishment from God. Only the woman who wished to share her voice was struck with this terrible disease. At this point, the issues become much clearer. God's words do not match God's action, and it seems that Moses and the later dominant tradition both desire for a clear statement of authority in ministry. Specifically, this tradition wishes to devalue Aaron's contributions and rule out any ministry by women. But the inconsistencies with the words and actions attributed to God show the problem quite clearly. Moses desires control, and wishes to force out this woman who wishes to proclaim the faith. In the minds of such leaders, the proclamation of faith must be limited and restricted, controlled by leaders who can then monitor and parcel divine revelation.

Miriam responds to the centrality of Moses' leadership not by questioning his right to lead, but by questioning his right to exclude her. This inquiry escalates into conflict with life and death results. Fortunately for Miriam, Aaron succeeds in intercession and her leprosy disappears within a week. But the damage is done. Once more, male resistance conflicts with female leadership, and male control wins. Moses forces Miriam's informed, vibrant, prophetic voice out of ministry, so that his own strident voice might be the only one heard. It still happens. It still happens.

Rahab's Unlikely Leadership

A Place in the Tradition

Rahab is a most unlikely hero for women who would be leaders and proclaim the faith (Joshua 2).[1] She was a foreigner, from the Canaanite city of Jericho. Worse yet, she was a prostitute, a member of an unclean and disrespected profession. Yet she became a role model, a person to be valued and emulated.[2]

Perhaps, before the discussion of Rahab starts in earnest, a word should be offered about prostitution. Quite possibly, Rahab was an innkeeper as well as prostitute. If so, then she owned a sizable piece of property that was, as we know, within the city walls of Jericho (Joshua 2:2, 6, 15). This made her a wealthy woman. Furthermore, she was independent. Very few women in the ancient world could make that claim. Rahab did not depend on a husband's or father's generosity for her livelihood. She earned it herself. This self-sufficiency, more so than her sexual practices, alienated her from the rest of society. The social structures of the day did not allow women to operate on their own, and thus she was relegated to the taboo position of prostitute. She was a woman outside the system, even though she could afford to live inside the wall.

Was Rahab of Jericho simply a sexual reprobate who happened to be used as a tool for Yahweh's purposes? She was a greedy woman, according to many of the popular interpretations, who manipulated the situation for her own continued security, even though that meant that she became a traitor to her own city. But, as we shall see, the story reads a bit differently than that.

A Place to Stay

The story begins as a spy tale. It's not the only spy story in the Old Testament, which gives us help in interpreting this particular one. Joshua was the newly appointed commander of the combined Israelite military forces, and his first objective was the capture of Jericho, which would be a key city near the center of the promised land, the capture of which would allow for further

---

[1]See Phyllis Bird, "The Harlot as Heroine: Narrative Art and Social Presupposition in Three Old Testament Texts," *Semeia* 46 (1989): 119–139.

[2]Along with Tamar, she joins the list of Jesus' ancestors (Matthew 1:5). According to this genealogy, Rahab is also Ruth's mother-in-law.

military campaigns. Joshua faced a problem, though; Jericho was exceptionally well-defended. So he sent spies into Jericho to investigate what was on the inside of the walls and find the sensitive spots where his forces could breach the fortifications. These spies infiltrated the city and spent the night in the local inn, which doubled as a brothel. There they met Rahab.

Prostitutes collected knowledge, in addition to their other roles. Rahab would have listened to the gossip from men of many different social locations throughout Jericho, and thus she would be a good source of information. But while the spies were at Rahab's place, the king of Jericho discovered that they were somewhere in the city. The king sent a contingent to search through Rahab's place, but she was successful in hiding them safely. Then, she gave them the information that they needed to make plans for conquest. Rahab betrayed her own city, but she had a loyalty deeper than that.

A True Faith

One might expect Rahab to act out of self-interest. Because she could see that her town was about to be invaded, she would help the potential conquerors in exchange for protection. If the walls held and Jericho stood, then Rahab would not have lost anything, but if the Israelites won, then she would still be alive, protected by the very soldiers who were destroying her city. It seemed a sensible bet no matter what happened. Certainly, it was the kind of bet that Jacob or Judah would have taken, since they always worked out of their own self-interest. Rahab was looking out for herself and her family; she had taken care of herself while in a rough profession, and she would take care of herself and her own no matter what else came her way.

Rahab did act in her own self-interest, but that was not the motivation that she explained to the Israelite spies. She proved herself to be a woman of faith and, in a sizable speech, she proclaimed that faith to the spies (Joshua 2:8–14). She preached proper worship of Yahweh to Israelite spies! Much of her discourse focuses on the historical doings of Yahweh, the sorts of things that would have made newspaper headlines in a more modern society. Sihon destroyed! Og leveled! But her proclamation of faith went beyond the immediate political concerns. She described Yahweh as God in heaven above and earth below (Joshua 2:11). Though this is not the most complex theological assertion ever made, she provided a clear theological rationale for her actions, and in doing so she proclaimed the faith.

In response to her faith in Yahweh, Rahab gave the spies advice that kept them alive and she hid them from the army of the king of Jericho when they stormed her place looking for the spies. She was faithful to them, and in turn she asked from them a price. Rahab requested asylum for herself and her family among the Israelites on the day that they defeated Jericho. She negotiated quite fairly with the Hebrew spies, offering them the protection and information that they needed and receiving in return a guarantee of safety during the battle and long-term security afterwards. When the Hebrew armies arrived and destroyed Jericho, they saved Rahab and her family, who then lived happily ever after among the Israelites (Joshua 6:22–25).

Understanding the Story

Many features of the story's meaning readily appear to the interpreter. Rahab is a woman rejected by her society, but she knows Yahweh and Yahweh's deeds, and so she betrays her city to maintain her loyalty to God. For this act and proclamation of faith, she receives a reward of a place within Israel for herself and her family. The story seems quite straightforward. But there's more to Rahab and her story than first meets the reader's eye.

A comparison of this spy tale with an earlier one heightens the sense of irony within the story. In the Rahab story, Joshua appears as Israel's chief military commander, though he has just taken the post and is now planning his first major campaign. In an earlier spy story, Joshua was the spy, on his first military mission. In Numbers 13, Moses sent twelve spies, including young Joshua, to spy throughout the promised land, which the Israelites would one day capture; the siege of Jericho would turn out to be the first concrete step toward that goal. Ten of the spies on that early trip reported that the Canaanites who lived in that land were undefeatable, but Caleb and Joshua argued that Israel could conquer Canaan, with God's help.

These two spy stories (Numbers 13 and Joshua 2) share many features in common. Both begin with a commissioning by a chief military official (Moses in the first story, Joshua in the second) and then tell of the spies' extensive journeying to find the needed information. Lastly, the spies return to their military commander, and report whether or not the Israelite army can defeat the occupants of the land. These stories are part of the same type of narrative. There is one other essential part of this type of story: the proof of the land's goodness.

Spies must perform two tasks in these stories: they must identify the benefits of the land and they must identify whether or not the inhabitants of the land can be conquered. Both tasks are absolutely imperative. Even if Israel could easily conquer the land with a minimum of loss, there would be no point in the attack if there was nothing in the land worthwhile. On the other hand, if the land is rich and bountiful, then the Israelite army might find reason to face tougher odds in their attempt to conquer. Thus, it is not enough for the spies to determine military capacity; they must also determine the goodness of the land. Furthermore, it is not enough that they assess the land's value. The spies must bring back *proof* that the land is worth taking.

In the earlier spy story, the twelve spies had searched through the land. They found one thing of great value that they could bring back to show everyone as proof of the land's bounty. What they found was a huge cluster of grapes. These grapes were so big that it took two of them to carry it, having lashed the grape cluster to a pole (Numbers 13:23). Those amazing grapes proved that the land was worth having. This fulfilled the first half of their task by giving evidence for the land's goodness. Everyone who saw those huge grapes growing in such abundance would be motivated to take the land as their own. All the Israelites would want to have those valuable grapes in the middle of their own community.[3]

But what did the two spies who visited Rahab find? The structure of the story demands that they find something of value that they can take back to their people. Furthermore, the story's structure requires that they find this valuable item *before* they assess the city's vulnerability to attack. We must look in the middle of the story for the proof of the city's value, and that leaves only one possibility: the thing of value is Rahab's testimony about God. For this reason, the spies reported back to Joshua that Jericho was worth having. Rahab's proclamation of faith was like abundant, succulent grapes; it was sweet and precious, capable of motivating a whole nation to take it into

---

[3] As the story turned out, the majority of spies felt that the land did not pass the second test of vulnerability, so the Israelites did not attack Canaan at that time, causing a long wait in the progress of history.

itself and to treasure it forever. Such is the power of women's testimony of faith, even when the woman is a traitor and a prostitute. The nature of the witness' background makes little difference in this story; the content of the proclamation makes all the difference in the world.

The prize to seek in the conquest of Jericho was the faith of this woman, and this prize was enough to motivate the people. With Rahab's practical assistance in assessing and circumventing the power of the Jericho forces and with the motivation of Rahab's faith, Joshua begins the plans for the conquest of Jericho.

An Uncontrollable Woman

More than Rahab's faith attracted these spies. They agreed to take Rahab and her family into the midst of the people of Israel. The story confirms that Joshua and the Israelites upheld their bargain: "Joshua let live Rahab, all her family, and everything that belonged to her. She has dwelled in the center of Israel until this day" (Joshua 6:25). But this is much more than upholding a bargain. So much popular interpretation has emphasized that the Israelites begrudgingly kept a bargain with an undesirable woman, but the structure of the story shows the truth of the situation. Rahab's faithful testimony to Yahweh was the proof of Jericho's worth, but it was much more than her proclamation of faith that Israel accepted into itself. Israel took Rahab into its center, just as earlier they had accepted magnificent grapes into their midst, because of Rahab's essential goodness and worth. They affirmed her as a valuable addition to their community, and the text even mentions that her family maintained a position of respect throughout Israel's history.

Rahab would be a dangerous addition to Israel. First of all, she was a foreigner, a Canaanite. The Israelites knew God's command to eradicate the Canaanites, but her proclamation of faith overruled any judgment that the community could pass against her. In their minds, Canaanites were not just an undesirable ethnic group, but a nation of degenerate sinners. Rahab should have been killed, but this woman's proclamation of faith disallowed any prejudice at all.

Secondly, Rahab's threat of treachery remained. She had sold out Jericho, and now Israel accepted a traitor into their midst. This made her a dangerous figure, with the constant possibility that she would change her loyalties again. In a time when standard military policy was the extermination of all possible threats, Joshua spared Rahab and let her live in the community's midst. Not only did Rahab live in Israel, but so did her family. They had made no statement of faith, but Rahab's faith carried a salvific force that spilled over onto them, allowing her family the ability to live with Israel as well. Her family may not have held their loyalty to Yahweh and Israel as Rahab did; they may have lost much more than she did in the destruction of Jericho. But her proclamation of faith saved her family.

Lastly, Rahab represented a continuing threat to the community because she was a prostitute. There is no indication that she gave up her business when she moved in among the Israelites. In fact, the text specifically says that Joshua spared all that belonged to her, and that may well have included her business. Prostitutes were dangerous figures for several reasons. Often, they contributed wrong religious influences to the Israelites. Rahab was a faithful worshipper of Yahweh while she was in Jericho, and yet she continued her life as a prostitute then; there seems no reason to think that the circumstances changed after Jericho's destruction. She still needed to make a living for herself. There is no indication from the story that Joshua required her to change her lifestyle or that Israel provided funds for her living without working.

Rahab the prostitute also endangered the entire economic system upon which ancient Israel was constructed. She was a working woman whose livelihood did not depend on a single man or family. Instead, she cared for her own family economically. Her role was to work for her own livelihood, and that sharply contradicted the cultural expectations for women.

Breaking the Monopoly of Order

Israel knew that Rahab represented a contradiction in several ways. She was a working woman who avoided pregnancy; she was a loyal traitor; she was an accepted prostitute; she was a Canaanite Israelite; she was a woman who proclaimed the faith. When they accepted Rahab, Israel welcomed these contradictions into their midst. Such radical contradictions would violate the common expectations and run the strong risk of breaking the monopoly of order. Israel in these early, formative years strove to unify itself and to produce one singular understanding of their identity. Such contradictions endangered their sense of self. Still, they accepted Rahab.

Bringing contradictions into one's deepest self in this fashion partakes of chaos.[4] Rahab's name is very similar to the Hebrew word for chaos, and perhaps the text expects the readers to make this connection. The Israelites take chaos into their midst and violate the order of the society. At a time when Israel desired to unify itself and when the men attempted an increasing monopoly on power, propriety, and order, they embraced chaos in the form of Rahab.

Rahab, then, serves as a permanent reminder of the value of chaos. The people from time to time must take chaos into themselves because of its inherent value. They should not always control or eradicate chaos, because through the breaking of rules and boundaries comes amazing possibilities for God's blessings. Had the Israelite spies never entered into this Canaanite prostitute's house, they never would have found the ecstasy of God's blessing, but Rahab gladly showed the spies the pleasures of a woman's proclamation of faith.

Israel gained immeasurably by taking chaos into itself. Rahab taught them an important lesson about the power of God to accept persons and to use them for God's purposes in the face of human prejudices and restrictions. Often, today's churches begrudge the inevitable disorder and change involved in including women and others who are not part of the existing power structure. Rahab's story points out the problem in such attempts to hold on to order at all costs. If such good can come from one chaotic woman who proclaimed the faith of Yahweh, how much more can come from the inclusion of women in the ministries of proclamation and action today?

---

[4]Process theology concerns itself with the bringing together of relationships within God's self, including the relationships that limited human perspectives would deem contradictory or disorderly. See Marjorie Suchocki, *God-Christ-Church: A Practical Guide to Process Theology* (New York: Crossroads, 1982).

Chapter **8**

Power and Powerlessness

How can women relate to power? What happens to women when men use power against them? What types of power can women use in the world? These questions, just like the questions about women's opportunities to proclaim the faith, are present in our time.

Our society still levels many devastating tirades against women who take control of their own lives, as did Potiphar's wife, Tamar, Miriam, and Rahab. When women attain power, the attacks against them can be even more disastrous. On the other hand, many women live without the power needed to change their situations or to control their circumstances, and they quickly become victims. Both power and powerlessness seem difficult for women; women risk loss through either means. Still, there must be some ways to attain power without misusing it or to turn powerlessness into some form of power.

The book of Judges offers four important stories about women and their lives with or without power. In those days, there were no kings in Israel, and so life was unpredictable and all too often violent. At one level, the whole book of Judges functions as a morality lesson about what can go wrong when there is not proper authority among the people. The question is one of power. Who has power? Is that power used in beneficial ways? Specifically, who benefits from the power? The book of Judges seems to argue that when there are no kings, then there is anarchy, where everyone has just enough power to misuse it but where no one has enough power to stop those who are dangerous. We will be in a better position to evaluate the larger questions of power after examining the stories of these five women: Deborah, Jael, Delilah, Jephthah's daughter, and a Levite's concubine. We shall focus on how they attained and used different kinds of power and how they lived with the lack of power.

Deborah and Jael: Military Power

Judging the People

The first story for our attention is that of the judge Deborah and her cohort Jael. This is an encouraging story for women (at least at the first reading) because here a woman, Deborah, takes the position of highest authority among the people, and another woman, Jael, takes direct action for which she receives great praise and honor. In those ancient days, there were no kings in Israel, and so the governmental organization was quite loose and flexible. When emergencies arose, then God would find a judge for the people. The term *judge* is a poor one for us, because it makes moderns think of our bureaucratic court systems where law is applied in small-scale situations typically to determine whether or not to incarcerate. Perhaps a better translation for the Hebrew term here would be "bringer of justice." Usually, these bringers of justice were military leaders who commanded the troops into battle. Once the threat to Israel was over, then the army disbanded and the bringer of justice went back to her or his other work. This system of leadership was always temporary, flexible, and rather informal, responding to the precise needs of the time.

Though most of the bringers of justice were men, one of the first was a woman, Deborah (Judges 4—5). At that time, Israel was under attack by Hazor, a Canaanite city whose armies marched behind their commander, Sisera. Deborah placed her armies under the command of her friend, Barak, and Deborah made plans for Barak to follow in the military engagement that was soon at hand. The battle went well for Barak's Israelite forces, and Sisera fled for his life to the tent of a woman named Jael, where he anticipated that he would be safe.

Deborah was ahead of Sisera. She knew of the plan and watched it come into being. Sisera asked Jael for asylum, and she granted it willingly. She fetched a drink for him and agreed to tell no one that he was there. But as the general Sisera slept, Jael walked up to him quietly, and pounded a tent peg through his skull, killing him. Then Jael turned the corpse over to Barak's army (Judges 4:17–22). The enemy was dead, and Israel was saved once more—this time, by the hands of two women, Deborah and Jael.

Murder

The story praises women's power. After the victory, Deborah and Barak sang a song of praise and celebration. The song praised Deborah.

> The rural people prospered;
> > in Israel they prospered,
> because Deborah arose,
> > arose as a mother for Israel.
> > > Judges 5:7

Deborah receives credit for her domestic administration. Under her leadership, the common folk of Israel received the economic benefits that allowed prosperity. This would not be wealth, but would be a sufficiency that would ease the cares of life. Her leadership is compared to that of a mother, because of her caring for all people and for their daily provision. These are high compliments for any political leader. Jael also receives extensive praise for her actions.

> May Jael be the most blessed of women,
> > she who is the wife of Heber the Kenite!
> May she be the most blessed among the nomadic women!
> For water he asked; milk she gave;
> > in a noble bowl she brought curds.
> She stretched out her hand to the tent peg,
> > and her right hand to the worker's hammer.
> She pounded Sisera; she crushed his head;
> > she broke and pierced his temple.
> Between her feet he collapsed;
> > he fell; he lay.
> Between her feet he collapsed;
> > he fell where he collapsed;
> > > there he fell, destroyed.
> > > > Judges 5:24–27

Jael is a military hero. Her acts in battle receive close, intense description that leaves no doubt as to the propriety of her use of power. She brought about the death of the enemy, and that makes her a genuine war hero. The singers do not discredit her at all just because her victory was achieved in covert military action rather than in open warfare.

Deborah, well into a helpful administration dealing with domestic issues, became the commander-in-chief of a massive and successful military campaign. She brought her people to military salvation. Jael, another woman, played a decisive role in the actual accomplishment. But Jael's means horrify: she drove a tent peg through the head of the sleeping general. For both of these different acts of power, these women receive men's praise.

Women's Power to Take Men's Power

Deborah demonstrates an ability to use men's power. Though the position of judge (or "bringer of justice") was typically a male role, she filled that position with distinction and with a great deal of success. It would not be exaggeration to suggest that many men had filled that post with fewer results. Deborah uses her power as judge to empower others, such as Barak and Jael, to perform their tasks. Deborah's power is cooperative power that enables others to work together with her toward the common goal.

Jael takes men's power in a different sense: she left Sisera powerless. Furthermore, Jael uses the same power that men typically use in warfare, which is the power to kill. In that sense, Jael uses a disempowering power. She renders her opponent helpless and then kills him. Jael's power is the opposite of Deborah's power. Deborah enables her colleagues to perform their tasks; Jael renders her opponent unable to perform his task, because she has killed him. Jael acts like a man in her use of power, taking power from another. Deborah works within a man's role, but administers that role in ways that are more distinctive to women, in that she encourages others to share her power.[1] For both of them, violence is a part of power, and they accept and welcome that part when they understand violence to be effective in reaching their goals of survival.

Delilah: Power to Destroy from Within

Samson

Samson was another one of Israel's judges (Judges 13—16). He was an extremely violent, uncontrollable man who made

---

[1]For a contrast, consider Samson, a judge who has a complete inability to work with others.

murder a hobby. He waged a one-man war against the Philistines, Israel's enemies. He was also a very colorful character,
whose deeds were often accompanied by riddles and unusual
acts.[2]

Samson's marriage celebration provides a wonderful example
of this judge's character. Though Israel's sworn enemies were the
Philistines, Samson decided to marry a Philistine woman. On his
way down to court her, he had met a lion along the road and he
had torn it apart with his bare hands, tossing the corpse aside.
Later, when he went to the wedding itself, he took a short detour
to see the lion. Its carcass had been infested with insects, including bees who had produced honey there, so he took out the
honey and ate some.

At the marriage celebration, he offered a riddle on the first
day of the week-long feast. It went like this: "Out of the eater
comes something to eat; from the strong comes something sweet"
(Judges 14:14). Samson made a bet with a group of the men
there that they could not guess the riddle by the end of the feast.
Of course, they couldn't, so they went to Samson's bride and
enlisted her aid in wheedling the answer out of Samson. She
discovered the truth after wearing him down with crying, and
then she told the men who had the bet with Samson.

When the men knew the answer, Samson knew that he had
been betrayed. He lost the bet and would have to pay thirty sets
of clothing. In great anger, he went to a nearby Philistine town
and killed thirty people, stealing the clothes from their
backs. He took the clothes back to the wedding feast, paid off
his wager, and kept on walking, leaving his bride alone at the
wedding.

Later, Samson rethought the situation, and went back to
claim his wife. When he found out that she had been given in
marriage to one of his friends, Samson captured three hundred
foxes, put torches on their tails, and released them through
Philistine fields, decimating their crops. When the town came out
to stop him, Samson killed them all, ripping them apart limb
from limb.

Samson's character exhibited an inability to form stable relationships, to put it lightly. His power was only a power to destroy,

---

[2]For a complete treatment of the Samson stories, see James L. Crenshaw,
Samson: A Secret Betrayed, A Vow Ignored (Atlanta: John Knox Press,
1978).

which he used repeatedly to kill Philistines. Unlike his predecessor Deborah, Samson showed no ability to build coalitions and share power.

Delilah

Once, Samson fell in love. Again, his object of desire was a Philistine woman, by the name of Delilah. The story is familiar. The Philistine leaders contacted Delilah and asked her to extract information from Samson, so that they could render him powerless. In the end, her undercover work succeeded, and the Philistines learned to shave Samson's head in order to remove his divine favor and thus his power. They then bound Samson and blinded him, imprisoning him for life as a sideshow attraction.

Delilah and Samson were a perfect match. Both used their power entirely to destroy. Samson fought battles externally, and he was unbeatable there. Delilah, on the other hand, used her power from the inside, where Samson had vulnerability. This gave her the advantage. Her power over Samson was strong, even stronger than this judge's legendary strength. She overpowered him.

Of course, Samson had power that he did not use against Delilah. His strength was physical, and he could have killed her with his bare hands at any point in the story. But he chose not to. At this one point in his life, if not at any other time, Samson chose to restrain his power, though it might have been better for him had he not done so. Delilah used all of her power against an enemy who used none of his, and so she overpowered him against all odds. An important part of power is knowing when to use some of it and knowing when to use all of it. At the end of his life, Samson decided, perhaps for the first time, to use *all* of his power, and it resulted in the death of many Philistines along with his own death. There is a price for using *all* of one's power.

Disloyalty and Destruction

Delilah and Samson could each destroy the other, Delilah through sabotage and Samson through physical strength. Delilah violated the relationship between them in order to use her power to destroy Samson through disloyalty. Her power took away Samson's power, just as his power of death would have taken away her power of deceit. The fact still remains that neither of them shows any potential for a positive power that would have empowered the other.

Whereas Deborah has power to destroy the body, Delilah uses her power in an attempt to destroy the soul, by going against the deepest religious convictions of Samson. Instead of using power for loyalty and for constructive purposes, Delilah's power degenerates into destruction.

Jephthah's Daughter: Power to Suffer Together

Jephthah's Story

Jephthah was another one of Israel's judges (Judges 11).[3] His story began with distress and descended into deep despair, driven by his own sense of powerlessness in the face of his past. Jephthah began life as the son of a prostitute and a man named Gilead. He was a mighty warrior, but he was an outcast because his mother was a prostitute. His brothers forced him off of the family property, and Jephthah found employment as a mercenary, where he gained fame and some measure of respect.

Israel's military situation again grew grim, and the elders of Jephthah's hometown sought him out and offered him the position of head of the local militia. Jephthah was incredulous. Why would they ask him back after years of rejecting him? A prophet has no honor in that prophet's hometown, and Jephthah was skeptical that a judge and a prostitute's son could find any honor there, either. Jephthah bargained for an even more important position as chief of the city, and the elders agreed. Their situation was desperate, and they perhaps would have agreed to anything. But the deed was done, and Jephthah took the people forward into battle.

God supported this battle. The narrator tells us specifically that "the spirit of Yahweh came upon Jephthah" (Judges 11:29). This gift of the spirit, however, was not enough for Jephthah. He had come from a rough background. His mother had given him up; his father never protected him; his brothers left him alone; his hometown kicked him out. More than anything else, Jephthah lacked trust, especially the trust of others that comes from self-

---

[3]For an extremely important treatment of this story, see Phyllis Trible, *Texts of Terror: Literary-Feminist Readings of Biblical Narratives* (Overtures to Biblical Theology, 13; Philadelphia: Fortress Press, 1984), pp. 93–116.

respect. So Jephthah tried to get a commitment from God. A gift of spirit, with its accompanying clear sense of God's approval for Jephthah and his actions, was insufficient; this man needed *proof*, so he made a vow.

Jephthah's vow contained portions for him and for Yahweh (Judges 11:30–31). Yahweh's task was to ensure the victory, which had already been promised. Jephthah's task would come only later; he wanted to see God's actions first. Jephthah promised to offer whatever he first saw coming out of his house when he returned home from the battle. When he returned victorious, his only daughter ran out to greet him, and he shouted at her with words of blame. Now he would kill his daughter.

Jephthah made a vow and kept it, even at the price of his daughter's death. On one level, this is a story about the importance of vows, just as the story of Samson concerned that judge's vow to keep his hair long. The crucial difference in the structure of the characters is that this woman, Jephthah's daughter, works to fulfill the vow whereas Delilah labored her strongest to negate Samson's vow. The difference in result, of course, is that the abrogation of Samson's vow causes his death, but the fulfillment of Jephthah's vow brings death not to himself but to his daughter.

The Daughter's Story

For Jephthah's young daughter, the story only began there. The battle had been a dangerous one, and she had probably worried whether or not her father would return. As far as the reader can be certain, her only motive in running out of the house as soon as she saw him was her joy in his return. Her vivacious greeting met harsh words of blame for her coming outside, and she learned quickly about the vow and her impending death.

She refused to bargain for her life or to try to avoid the death sentence of the vow. Instead, she requested a space of time, two months, to go into the hills where she could be alone with her women friends. Then, she would come down from the hill and submit to her execution. This embodies two concepts of power that have not been before. First, there is the power to submit. She will perform the deed, but on her terms and at her timing, not her father's. Though this is an important form of power, it still results in death, though perhaps it changes slaughter to death with dignity, depending upon perspective. Second, there is quite strongly the power of the community of women.

Jephthah's daughter knows what she does and does it willingly and intentionally. She works within a very different concept
of power than Deborah or Delilah, both of whom see power
strictly as ways to make things happen to *other* people.

The Power of Women Affirmed

The daughter knows the power of solidarity with her sisters,
and the statement of this power is most significant. After two
months within a community of women, she will be empowered to
face anything. The congregation of women empowers its members because of its support of each one there as a person and as
a woman.

This time with the women outside the village may reflect an
actual practice. The story itself provides the reader with that clue,
because it refers to a continuing practice in commemoration of
Jephthah's daughter. The other clue comes in the words of her
request: she asks for time to mourn her *betulah* with her women
friends. This Hebrew term has traditionally been translated as
"virginity," with the understanding that she wishes time to cry
over the fact that she will never enjoy marriage or sex. But
betulah is more specifically an age designation during which
young women may marry. She requests time to express her
feelings about her age. This may reflect a practice of a lengthy
rite of initiation for women at the start of menstruation.[4] There are
indications within the Old Testament that women had a special
place outside the border of the camp or village where they spent
the times of their menstruation.[5] This women's place may be
where Jephthah's daughter goes at this time. Within those two
months, the women of the community would pass through the
women's place, forming a consistent yet shifting community.[6]
There, she could experience the company of women in affirming,

---

[4]For a closely related thesis, see Peggy L. Day, "From the Child Is Born
the Woman: The Story of Jephthah's Daughter," in *Gender and Difference in
Ancient Israel*, ed. Peggy L. Day (Minneapolis: Fortress Press, 1989), pp.
58–74. Day deals with evidence from other cultures as well.

[5]Cp. Leviticus 12's impurity laws with the treatment of various areas
outside the camp in Leviticus 13:46; 14:39–47; Numbers 5:1–4; 31:19; and
Deuteronomy 23:10–13.

[6]Not all women would have visited the women's place; only those
menstruating would have done so. This would exclude children and
postmenopausal women (the few who had survived childbirth), as well as
pregnant women and those immediately *postpartum*.

life-giving ways. This group of women, regardless of their specific reason for gathering, is a powerful entity, and their power empowers her for the task ahead of her.

The Powerlessness of Men

Despite his emotion for his daughter, Jephthah cannot see past the words of the vow. He does not seem able to value life and to know that God values life more than vows. The words of his faith have locked him in tightly, and he has lost grasp of the essence of faith. In this sense, Jephthah is quite powerless to even consider other options. He does not even have the power to see that God gave the victory before the vow; God never desired this absurd vow in the first place.

Jephthah still retains the power to destroy his daughter's life, but he never had the power to take her memory. That memory is now bound up in the life of the women's community who mourn together the destructive excesses of male power and powerlessness. Like far too many others in these stories, Jephthah's only power is to destroy. In the end, he even lacks the power to save himself from complicity in this tragedy that he is about to commit.

The story has a strange effect on the reader. As I read it, I want to scream to her to run away, to avoid that wrongful death as an innocent victim and to avoid it at any cost. Perhaps that is one of the effects of this story; it makes the reader realize how wrong the abuse of women is, and how easily we hide that abuse behind mechanisms of control, such as vows, and anger that blames the victim, as happened here.

Like Tamar, Jephthah's daughter takes matters into her own hands, though with greatly different results. She walks willingly to her death, and we readers may still pray that her sacrificial death teaches us something, and in some odd way brings us life through her willing death. If not, it is only a senseless tragedy, but if the story does bring life, then her death has real, saving power—even if only the salvation of a piercing, disturbing scream.

A Levite's Concubine:
Powerlessness and Meaninglessness

The book of Judges ends with a truly horrible story (Judges 19—21).[7] The story begins with a Levite, who would be a mem-

---

[7]See the classic study by Phyllis Trible, *Texts of Terror*, pp. 65–91.

ber of one of the categories of the priesthood. This man had a concubine. In the story, neither this man nor this woman receive names. After a serious yet unspecified disagreement, the woman left the man, and went back to her father's household. The man made no attempts to retrieve her until some four months later, when he made a trip down to her hometown of Bethlehem. He bargained with her father to take her back home with him. The father agreed, but seemed to stall the return. Five days later, the man had waited long enough and insisted on leaving immediately. Even though it was the end of the day, he reasoned, they could at least get a few miles down the road, and perhaps stay in Jebus, the city that David would later rename Jerusalem. So the man and the woman finally started on their postponed reunion journey, and they arrived later that night in the Canaanite city of Jebus.

Already, the story has developed several unresolved problems. Why did this Levite take a concubine instead of marrying her outright, since there seems not to be a wife in the picture? What was their disagreement? If it was her fault, why was *she* the one to leave? Why did he neglect her for most of a year and *then* seek her out? Why did the man and the woman not speak during their time in Bethlehem? Could their relationship ever restore itself if they did not talk the problems through? If the father supported the reunion, why did he delay things so many times? What was the Levite's hurry? All these questions stack up; they resonate with each other and take on added strength in their numbers. The story sets itself up for failure; there are too many unknowns and not enough discussion of the *real* problems for any assurance that things will turn out well. On the other hand, nothing really wrong has happened yet, so maybe we readers should not jump to conclusions. But if we did think that things were about to become disastrous, our expectations would not be disappointed. Not at all.

Past Jerusalem and on to Gibeah

Near Jerusalem, things went poorly for this man and woman so recently reunited. The man and his servant discussed the issue. The servant thought that they should stay in Jerusalem, since it was right at hand, but the man thought that they should go on a few more miles through the dark, until they reached Gibeah. After all, he reasoned, Gibeah is Israelite territory, and

Jerusalem is Canaanite. Who knows what could go wrong in Canaanite lands?

When the traveling party reached Gibeah, it was already too late at night for anyone to be about on the streets. Finally, they found an old man who agreed to take them in for the night (Judges 19:16–21). Off they went to his house. But there were sounds outside that threatened to overtake the serenity within that house. Soon, a large group of the townsmen pounded on the old man's door, demanding that he release the man so that they could rape him. The old man, thinking of the requisite hospitality, refused to send out the man, but offered the man's concubine and the old man's virgin daughter as objects of rape. Before the crowd could respond, the Levite threw his concubine out the door. Through the night, the whole town raped her and beat her. Shortly before dawn, she crawled to the door of the old man's house.

When the Levite opened the door in the morning, he found her lying on the doorstep. She didn't respond to his forceful commands to get up, so he put her on the back of his donkey and took her to his house, a few days ride away. Once there, he went inside and got his knife, and he cut her into twelve pieces and sent a chunk of her corpse to each of Israel's tribes, requesting counsel.

We are shocked to realize that the text never tells us plainly that she died as a result of that night of vicious, abusive gang rape. Did he find her corpse on the doorstep, and ride those several days through the hot sun with a dead and broken body tied behind him on the donkey? Or did he kill her himself at his house as an object lesson, disregarding the law about murder in the same way that we know he disregarded the customs about burial? We will never know; whether dead or alive, she was silent.

No matter how the death occurred, the scene ends in death. The Levite, supposedly a religious leader and an example for the people, protects himself at the price of his concubine's life. The people of Gibeah, supposedly Israelite and thus morally superior to the Jebusites, commit the atrocity of gang rape and physical torture, perhaps culminating in death. The concubine was power-less in the face of her attackers, and her powerlessness ended in death, the ultimate lack of power.

Contagious Death

The Levite did not stop there. Before he was done, the death would spread in ever increasing circles. All the Israelites from all the tribes gathered to discuss this atrocity (Judges 20:1–11). The Levite presented his case, clarifying that the men of Gibeah had raped her to death, and conveniently avoiding any mention of his own role in throwing her out into their midst. Israel decided that Gibeah deserved punishment, so they formed an army of 400,000 to attack Gibeah's force of 26,000, which was augmented with the men from the tribe of Benjamin. Within the first two days of battle, Israel lost 40,000 with hardly a loss on Gibeah's side. But the battle turned on the third day, and Israel's losses totaled only thirty, but they decimated Gibeah and the tribe of Benjamin, killing 25,100 out of their 26,000 fighting men (Judges 20:29–34). This near extermination of the tribe of Benjamin could only be termed an atrocity of war, just as the concubine's rape and murder was itself an atrocity. Death spreads.

Israel again gathered. They did not wish to rid themselves of one of their own tribes of kin. But Benjamin was almost dead, and the other eleven tribes had agreed not to give any of their women in marriage to Benjaminites. This would make the crucial task of repopulation virtually impossible. Israel sought a solution that would restore Benjamin, and they thought until they realized that one city had not sent any warriors to the coalition against Benjamin. That town was Jabesh-Gilead. Then Israel formed a plan. They sent 10,000 warriors against the peaceful, undefended city of Jabesh-Gilead, and they killed all the males plus all the adult women. All that was left of Jabesh-Gilead were 400 virgins, and Israel sold them to Benjamin as the price of the peace (Judges 21:1–12). Death spreads again.

However, 400 women were not enough for Benjamin, since they had at least 900 men left. So Israel arranged another attack. When the people gathered for the annual religious festival at Shiloh, Israel would allow the Benjaminites to attack and seize any of the virgins engaging in the liturgical dances of the ceremony. This kidnapping and forced marriage restored Benjamin to adequate population numbers, allowing them to restore their tribe. The only price was the violation of the people's highest religious festival, killing its sanctity. Death spreads again.

Through the story, Israel keeps trying to use power to solve its problem, but every application of power leads only to death. Death gives birth to death, growing with every generation. The Levite infected the world with death when he cast out the woman into the street with no protection, relinquishing, in a singularly selfish act, his power to care and love, his power to give life. Then, the Levite infected all of Israel with contagious death by sending out the chunks of her corpse. Once Israel caught this horrible malady, death rode wild throughout the entire people. No one seems to have had the power—or the sense—to stop the epidemic before tens of thousands were killed and hundreds more women were abandoned to serve as other's objects of sex. Death spread throughout the body.

The Story's Ending

How does the story end? It depends. It depends on who you are.

For the narrator, the story ends with a summary line for the whole book: "In those days, there was no king in Israel; each individual did what appeared right in that one's eyes" (Judges 21:25).[8] The narrator understands this story as an object lesson about the evils of anarchy, and it appears that the narrator claims to know a solution. If Israel had had a king, the narrator suggests, none of this would have happened. The answer is more authority. But one wonders. Certainly this anarchy was horrid, but would monarchy be any better? Would royal authority deliver any better results than this radical dispersion of power throughout Israel? It seems as if the deeper problem was what people do with power, not who held that power.

For the Benjaminites, the survivors of the tribe end the story in decent condition. They had lost almost all of their relatives, with less than four per hundred left alive. Despite the loss, the survivors gained the tools and the space within Israel to rebuild. They had to live in the shadow of this horrible atrocity, but at least they could live. Most of this story's characters never left the tale alive.

For the women of Jabesh-Gilead and of Shiloh, the story trailed away into nightmares of repeated loss of independence and dignity. They had lost their families and their abilities to stay in their homeland, to maintain their joint identity, and to express their opinions about a husband. They were captured, seized, kidnapped, and then subjected to some man's sexual desires. They were moved as a group into a strange territory, never to return to their homes and never allowed to bury their butchered loved ones. They only served to increase the numbers of a tribe

---

[8]The book of Judges repeats this refrain frequently.

with a history of abusing women, as they did to the Levite's concubine, and defending that abuse, as they did against Israel's armies. The women of Jabesh-Gilead and of Shiloh faced life within that environment every day of the rest of their lives, as far too many women do today.

For the Levite, the story ended in a complete loss of control. For him, the story began when he lost control of his concubine, and he lost control on an ever larger scale throughout the story. By the middle of the narrative, he disappeared; things had progressed completely beyond his capacity to cope. Repeatedly, he tried to gain power, but he lost control. Like so many other women and men in the book of Judges, his power was only a power to destroy, and so he remained incapable of controlling situations or improving life for anyone, even himself. One can imagine this Levite moving slowly to the background, observing the growing carnage in horror, wondering how it all got so bad and knowing that he could not do a thing about it.

For the concubine, the story ended early with rape, torture, and death. No one in the rest of the story does anything to redeem her death. Everyone tried to do something, but nothing really addressed the problem of the atrocity done against this woman. Besides, any solution would have been too late for her; she was already dead. She was completely silent and utterly powerless in the face of men's power to destroy; she died a horrible death utterly devoid of meaning.

Power and Authority: A Search for Meaning

What does this story mean? Can there be any meaning within such tragedy?

The story discusses power. When this woman was stripped of her power through her concubinage, death began. At first, her powerlessness brought the little death of a loss of self-identity and the rise of silence. Then, her powerlessness resulted in her own meaningless death. Finally, her powerlessness caused mass murder. Powerlessness is death, especially women's powerlessness. Frustratingly, men's power also leads to death, especially the death and devastation of women, over and over again.

The story also discusses unity and division. The book of Judges tries to argue for a monarchy as a preferable alternative to anarchy, but this story argues in the opposite direction. When the man and the woman were torn asunder, each was safe. When they were reunited, death soon followed. The men of Gibeah united, only to do evil and bring death. The men of Israel united, only to announce a policy of genocide and to enforce it with might. Later, the men of Israel united again, to condemn more men to death and to consign more women to loss of identity and self-determination. Division hardly seems the answer, either; the woman's body was divided and distributed, but no salvation came of that. Her division brought about male unity, and death spread.

Together, these four stories in the book of Judges paint a dire portrait of power. Perhaps we can gather the meaning only when we take them in reverse order. The powerlessness of the Levite's concubine resulted in her victimization. A strong message out of this story is that powerlessness is destructive, and woman's powerlessness leads to her death. As much as we might hate to admit it, only the strong survive. Women must have power and use it in order to live in such a world. In that light, the other acts of power appear much more attractive. Delilah's power was an almost completely negative power to destroy, and so it still depicts for us the dangers of power, but the other two stories teach important lessons about the value of women's power.

For Jephthah's daughter, women's community provided a power to accept. Perhaps that community should also have mustered a power to object, to oppose, to resist, to refuse, and thus to change and to give life. At least that community empowered this woman to meet death with some sort of meaning, whereas the woman in Judges 19—21 died without meaning at all. For Jael, her power to deceive and to kill enabled victory, and thus receives a much more positive evaluation. She used just the right amount of power at just the right time. Though we should still have difficulty with murder for any cause, Jael refrained from any excess and worked toward a goal of removing oppression. In light of the other options available to women later in the book of Judges, Jael's use of power deserves our admiration. Deborah's power empowered others around her to do their tasks with greater effect. She brought domestic tranquility and ensured Israel's peace. She is truly great among Israel's women, and greatly to be praised.

We should not leave without mentioning one other facet of women's power in this book. The book of Judges is full of death; people have died in each of the stories we have investigated. But women's power minimizes death. Under Deborah, the most powerful of these women, Sisera's death alone turned the tide and brought life to all Israel. In the case of the least powerful of these women, the Levite's concubine, her death and dismemberment triggered the eruption of civil war that nearly passed over into genocide. In the stories where women had the most power and held positions of the greatest authority and general respect, the people held back the forces of death, but when the society deprived women of power, death spread unchecked.

Though the book of Judges explains in painful detail the problems encountered when proper authority is missing from the people, another lesson echoes throughout these stories. Is life any better when there is a king? Perhaps life is only better when there is a God whom the people follow. As seen in the next chapter, monarchy rarely solves anything, nor does any other form of human authority, especially those based on the male power to destroy.

Chapter 9

Women
of the
Early Monarchy

In the story of the Levite's concubine, the traveling party avoided the city called Jebus, because it was a Canaanite town. After David became king, he conquered Jebus, renamed it Jerusalem, and made it his capital, uniting the political and religious leadership of the whole nation at that one place in the center of all the tribes (2 Samuel 5—6). With the last bastion of Canaanite life in Israel's midst defeated and the Philistine enemies to the southwest under check, Israel began a new phase of its existence. The period of early Israel was over, and the monarchy now ruled. This meant numerous changes in the lives of all Israelites, including the lives of Israelite women. Urbanization caused a large number of these changes.

Early Israel's existence was rural; the people were farmers and probably most of them were subsistence farmers. Men and women, both as adults and as children, worked together to eke out their existence from small plots of hilly land, making barely enough to keep them alive from year to year. The continuation of the Israelites always depended upon many factors. If crops were good one year, then their chances would increase. But there were many other things that could go wrong, such as plague, famine, bad weather, infestations, and raids. Any of these problems could create a huge problem for a family or a village; more than one at once would cause a disaster, possibly over a larger region or even a whole tribe. Life was always marginal for these early Israelites, in two senses: they lived on the edges of Canaanite city-states, and they lived just a little bit away from impoverished starvation and death.[1]

Life changed under the monarchy. The Canaanites either vacated their cities or began to coexist peacefully. Under David's reign, the former inhabitants of the land became Israelite, and "Israel" became the name of a nation with geographic boundaries, not just a term for a hillside, rural lifestyle with some loose ethnic connections living in the midst of others. David's control of the city-states was crucial to this endeavor, and soon city life became the dominant Israelite experience. Jerusalem, the new capital, became the focus of David's activity, as well as the religious center for the worship of Yahweh. Both politics and religion increasingly became urban endeavors. Since most of the writing of the Old Testament came from the dominant Jerusalem-based priests and scribes, these city experiences shaped the Old Testament. The traces of urban thought have already been seen in the stories investigated so far, but urban influences will become more dominant through the rest of this study.[2]

Urbanization also meant the rise of centralized authority. Before the monarchy, the Israelites were widely dispersed. Each family was mostly self-sufficient, though there were a large number of interconnections between the villages and the tribes. Once centralization changed the organization of life, the cities became the hub of activity. More people lived in the cities, buying their food from rural farmers. Trade became more important as individuals tended to specialize their activities. People no longer produced all the goods needed to live; instead, each family would make some things to consume themselves and some to sell elsewhere for the money to buy the things that they themselves did not produce. This created a rising merchant class, which dealt mostly in money instead of barter only, because they lived off the profits from their sales of other people's products. The leaders of the city became increasingly influential in the affairs of the rural folk, because city dwellers set the prices for rural goods. Protection against raiders was also centralized into a standing army, created for the first time in Israel's history under David.

---

[1]For a recent treatment of the early Israelite period, see Robert B. Coote, *Early Israel: A New Horizon* (Minneapolis: Fortress Press, 1990).

[2]For more technical considerations, see Norman K. Gottwald, *The Tribes of Yahweh: A Sociology of the Religion of Liberated Israel, 1250-1050 B.C.E.* (Maryknoll, New York: Orbis Books, 1979).

This centralized army was supported by the taxes of city dwellers and rural folk alike, and was one of the best examples of specialization and centralization.

In the years when David was king, things changed for everyone, especially women. For rural women, life may have continued in more or less the same fashion, but the economic shifts would have changed their lifestyles as well. No longer was their handiwork as essential to the family's survival, since more and more products could be purchased in the cities. Women's tasks emphasized childbirth more and more, and there was a decreased need for women's other work.

For the city dwellers, farming was no longer "women's work"; they were increasingly limited to the house. These city women were married to professionals who earned the money to buy the family's needs, and so these women stayed home and cared for the children, rarely leaving their houses. Perhaps in the old days of the rural lifestyle, women saw each other constantly as they worked together in the fields, surrounded by family and neighbors. Now, they might meet at the well, but not often elsewhere. Women did not gather to do their work together, though there were still some more limited times in the marketplace and in other corporate tasks. The city created women who were increasingly isolated from other adult women,and whose social life shifted toward an increasing emphasis on husband and children.

From this period come several important portraits of women. Three of these stories deal with David's wives, and one deals with David's daughter.[3] The last story tells of one of David's advisers. Together, these women represent only a small group of women, because these are all urban elites, most of whom are even members of the royal family. Yet they depict the changes that were taking place throughout the country as monarchy brought in urbanization and centralization.

Michal

From David's early years come stories of strong women, before the cities domesticated and victimized women to even greater extents. One of these first stories was about Michal. She

---

[3]For more detail on David's wives, see Adele Berlin, *Poetics and Interpretation of Biblical Narrative,* Bible and Literature Series (Sheffield: Almond Press, 1983).

was the daughter of Saul, Israel's first king. This story began as a love story, but soon became entangled in political machinations.

Michal loved David (1 Samuel 18:20). This pleased Saul, but for the wrong reasons. He was not happy with his daughter's happiness; he was looking for a way to trap David. Saul saw early on that David was rising to be the next king, and Saul fought against David in a variety of indirect ways. David was far too popular for Saul to risk assassination, but he desired other ways to remove or control this rival for his throne. Michal provided a means to control David, and so Saul encouraged the marriage. Saul followed the ancient proverb to hold one's friends close and one's enemies even closer. As David's father-in-law, Saul would hold him very close indeed.

David was young but not naive, and so he had misgivings about the marriage. He seemed quite pleased with Michal herself, but he claimed that he did not feel worthy to be Saul's son-in-law. After all, David was just a commoner, and could not afford the price to buy Michal as his wife. When Saul saw the possibilities for the marriage dwindling, he made another proposal: David could forego a cash bride price, and could substitute one hundred Philistine foreskins. David accepted the deal. Saul intended David to get himself killed in this endeavor, since it would be nearly impossible for any warrior, no matter how great, to kill one hundred Philistines. But David succeeded, and he took Michal as wife and became Saul's son-in-law (1 Samuel 18:20–28).

The rivalry continued and escalated to the point where Saul was ready to try outright murder. At that turning point, Michal decided to defy her father and act in loyalty to her husband, David. She helped David escape through a window, and she stayed behind in her father's house to cover up David's getaway (1 Samuel 19:8–17). This separated these young lovers for years; in the royal courts of the early monarchy, love often gave way to other factors, such as political necessity. Saul gave no thought to his daughter's love for David; when it seemed expedient, he married her to another man, named Palti (1 Samuel 25:44). Her feelings were never considered. It was Saul's choice to marry his daughter to whomever he pleased, and so he did.

After Saul's death, David worked to get Michal back. Though he had other wives by that time, he still desired to have her. But what were his motives? Did David still love her, or did he see the obvious benefits to uniting Israel's two royal lines into one? If David and Michal had a son, that boy would be the son of a king and the grandson of a king, and the lineage of royalty would be clearly established. David's motives were unclear, but he worked to bring Michal back to him (2 Samuel 3:13–16). Likewise, we cannot determine how Michal felt about David after these many years of separation. When a general kidnapped Michal to take her to David, her husband Palti cried bitterly, but we are never told if Michal cried or not. Perhaps she did weep out of her grief at losing Palti; perhaps she rejoiced at reunion with David, the love of her youth. Unlike the clear ardor of the first scenes, we do not know why David and Michal rejoin.

We do not know their expectations, but we know the end of David and Michal's relationship. Soon after Michal came to David, the king moved the ark into Jerusalem, and in the accompanying ceremony he danced vivaciously. Michal saw the dancing, and thought that it was unbecoming of a king. They argued, and David refused to see her again. Michal finished her days in the king's house with no access to David and with no children (2 Samuel 6:20–23).

Perhaps this argues for David's political motivations for re-uniting with Michal. He did not want any of Saul's heirs around. Any of Saul's heirs would be possible rivals to David's throne, and like Saul, David holds his potential enemies very close indeed. The scenes with Michal are full of emotional language; Michal loved David (1 Samuel 18:20, 28) and Palti loved Michal (2 Samuel 3:16). But the stories never attribute any emotion to David. The king was placid, and perhaps even uncaring; he desired political advantage, and marriages that sped his rise to power were appreciated. But there was no such thing as marriage for love or for happiness in David's life.

Abigail

For several years before becoming king, David was a ruffian in the wilderness areas between Israel and Philistia. For part of this time, he ran protection schemes. He and his mercenary band would guard someone's fields for a while, and then start asking them for payment in return. It made for a decent living in between the raids on Philistine towns for plundering. Once, David and his band of men offered this protection scheme to a rich man named Nabal, who refused. The reader should not express surprise at this act, because the name *nabal* means "fool." Certainly, refus-ing a mob's protection is always a dangerous act, if not actually foolish. Incensed, David ordered an attack on Nabal's house (1 Samuel 25:9–13). David's intentions receive only hints, but he clearly intended to kill all of the house's men and probably also planned to take the women and pillage the house. After all, that was what raiding bands usually did.

Nabal's wife, Abigail, heard about his arrogant refusal and instantly made plans. She gathered up enough for a good-sized feast and took it to meet David on the path. When they met, she apologized for Nabal and begged David's forgiveness (1 Samuel 25:18–31). Her quick action saved Nabal and his household. Later, Abigail told Nabal about all of this, and he slipped into a coma, from which he died in ten days. David heard of Nabal's death, and offered to marry Abigail.

When men play games of death, women struggle to survive. David indirectly murdered Abigail's husband, and yet she goes to marry him. Likely, she inherited none of Nabal's wealth, and there is no record that she had any sons to support her. Nabal's death left Abigail destitute, and David took advantage of that situation. Abigail's comment upon receiving the offer of marriage is that she was just a slave to wash feet (1 Samuel 25:41); she knew that she was in no position to argue.

Bathsheba

Though Michal and Abigail were important figures in David's early history, the best known story of David's wives deals with Bathsheba. Her name has entered the public imagination, and not the others, for two good reasons. First, the Bathsheba story is the most carefully told of the stories of David's wives. It makes a better movie and captures the attention with its seduction, intrigue, and murder. Second, Bathsheba was the wife who turned out to be the most important politically. Though she was not the first wife, nor the wife with the best political connections, she was the Queen Mother; her son, Solomon, was the one who finally took over his father's throne as King of Israel.

The story of Bathsheba and David strikes an ominous note from its beginning. In spring, when kings went out to war, David sat at home and sent his general to take care of that for him. So David had nothing to do, really, except sit on his roof and look around (2 Samuel 11:1–2). The message is so clear that it hits the reader between the eyes: David was not doing the things that kings are supposed to do. He wasn't busy being king. Trouble soon followed.

David noticed a beautiful woman from his lofty perch on top of the palace, and he sent after her. When she came to him, he consummated his lust with her, and then sent her away, not expecting to see her again (2 Samuel 11:3–4). Immediately, we have learned the character of the king: he avoids his work and he takes what is not rightly his. Before Saul became king, the prophet and judge Samuel had told the Israelites that kings would take everything the people had as their own, and David now had set about fulfilling that prophecy (1 Samuel 8:10–18). He sent others to war and took the remaining women for himself, without regard to their situations. The king uses people for his own benefit.

The story might have ended right there. Other days would come, the king's eye would wander in other directions, and then other women would feel the heat of the king's desire. But the story goes on. Before too many weeks had passed, while the army was still out to battle, Bathsheba sent a message to David: "I'm pregnant" (2 Samuel 11:5).

David panicked. It was one thing for a king to sleep around, but it would be another problem altogether if the word got around. Bathsheba's husband could surely count, and when he arrived home from a four-month absence, for instance, to a wife who was two months pregnant, bad things would happen. So the king hatched a plot. He recalled Bathsheba's husband, Uriah, from the battlefield. David thought that giving the poor bloke a few days' leave back at home would allay the future suspicions about the parentage of Bathsheba's child. Sure, she might still claim that it really was the king's child, but who would believe her?

Uriah foiled David's plot. Uriah was a faithful, pious man, who refused the comforts of home when his compatriots were in the midst of a war. Uriah refused to see his own wife, because of his loyalty to the troops. The text's shrewd criticism of David could not be stronger. Uriah would not sleep with his own wife because it was spring and it was time to be at war, but David would not only sleep with his own wives, but with Uriah's wife, too. Uriah was more righteous than David, but David would not admit it.

So David's cover-up entered its second phase. The king's power was a power to destroy, and so David sent a message, by Uriah's own hand, back to the front: Get Uriah killed! Joab, David's general, took the matter to heart. Now, Joab always went the next step. If asked to carry something one mile, he would go two, or even three. Joab never considered doing anything half-way. When Joab received the request to murder Uriah, he must have realized that this was part of a cover-up, and so he did it right. Joab had a large number of his soldiers killed in battle through intentionally poor military strategy (2 Samuel 11:14–25). David could not complain at Joab's overzealousness.

Bathsheba mourned her husband for a decent length of time, and then David requested her to marry him, apparently before she was even showing. The king was quick about such things, needless to say. It seemed as if the cover-up would succeed in the end, until the prophet Nathan walked into David's throne room one day and explained that he knew about the whole situation. God's response to the crimes of adultery and murder was the death of the child.

The text concentrates on David's reaction to the loss of the child, but in the background, Bathsheba cried. She had been used by the king, and she cried about that. She had lost her husband in a tragic accident—or *was* it an accident?—and she cried about that. She had been moved out of her home and into a stranger's house, and she cried about that. She had been forced into marrying a greedy little man who already had multiple wives, one of whom was a jilted princess, and she cried about that. Now, she had lost her firstborn, and no one even seemed to care what *she* thought of it, and she cried bitterly about that.

She cried over all that she had lost. A year later, David thought that the new baby, named Jedidiah or Solomon, took away all the pain, but it didn't. Bathsheba began as an innocent, but her victimization cost her her faithful husband and her first-born son. Jerusalem life, with its monarchy and urbanization, had taken its toll on women very quickly. Bathsheba lost every right and every piece of self-determination that she had ever had. David's adultery would never have happened before. In the old days, no able-bodied man would have been napping in the middle of the day with nothing to do. No woman would have been limited to her house, sealed away from other women whose company could have saved her. No military leader would have stayed home from the war. No buildings would have allowed the glimpse taken by that perverted watcher. No structure of author-ity could have executed her Uriah. Urbanization and centraliza-tion exacted a price, and Bathsheba, like so many women, paid dearly.

Bathsheba learned the system of the monarchy. She was present in the beginnings of David's time as monarch, and she observed how things ran over the years. She also had the benefit of outliving many of her colleagues in the royal court. Eventually, she became one of the chief advisers to David. There she earned the trust and admiration of the prophet Nathan, and together they engineered the coup that brought Solomon into the monarchy himself (1 Kings 1:15–27). As Queen Mother, she could use the system to her own advantage. Because she had gained power over the years, she could overcome her victimization and make sure that she never lost so much again. But nothing brought back her first, dead child or her first, dead husband. David was still the murderer who had taken them from her, no matter what else he had given over the years.

Tamar

David had a daughter, and through her story we learn that women did not fare well in the next generation of David's family, either. This daughter's name was Tamar, and she was Absalom's sister (2 Samuel 13).[4] Like almost everyone in these stories, Tamar was beautiful, and so her half brother Amnon desired her. Like father, like son, it seems. Amnon searched out some advice about how to handle this, and his cousin and good friend, Jonadab, provided a plan. If Amnon would play sick, then he could trick Tamar into bringing him his meals, and that would give him the opportunity to take advantage of her.

In retrospect, it must have seemed a stupid idea. After all, it might be a way to get alone and within arm's reach of Tamar, but there was no escape plan. If Tamar also wanted Amnon, how could they ever express it, because they were brother and sister? And if Tamar resisted, how could Amnon ever escape his father's wrath? But so many plans seem more solid before their initiation, and Amnon's lust was so strong that it overpowered reason. The plot proceeded.

Soon, Amnon had Tamar within his grasp. She pleaded for him to release her, begging him to realize what this would do to her, and even suggesting that David would agree to their mar-

---

[4]Phyllis Trible, *Texts of Terror: Literary-Feminist Readings of Biblical Narratives* (Overtures to Biblical Theology, 13; Philadelphia: Fortress Press, 1984), pp. 37-63, discusses this story with her usual detail and acuity.

riage if only he would go through the proper channels first (2 Samuel 13:12–13). Amnon would have none of that; he raped her. Afterwards, his feelings changed, and he hated her thoroughly (2 Samuel 13:15). The law would have given them an opportunity to marry, but he sent her away, dooming her to a life without marriage and thus without security or fulfillment.[5]

Tamar went to her brother, Absalom. This news kindled anger deep within him, and he plotted how to kill Amnon (2 Samuel 13:20–39). David, however, did nothing. This atrocity grew in dimensions, racing throughout the royal family like a blood-poisoning infection streaking away from a wound. First Amnon raped Tamar, then Absalom killed Amnon, then Absalom rebelled against David, then David had Absalom killed. The king could not control his own family, and he nearly lost the kingdom. Evil raged throughout the family and throughout the nation.

Tamar learned an important lesson through this event, and that lesson would soon become known throughout the kingdom. No woman can trust the king for protection, not even his own daughter.[6]

The Tekoite Woman

After Absalom murdered Amnon, Absalom fled from David. After a while, David forgave the murder, and he wanted his son Absalom back with him, but David was afraid of what people would think (2 Samuel 13:37–39). Instead of acting out of forgiveness, David kept his feelings bottled inside and let it eat away at him. This certainly was typical of David; his power included only the power to destroy and to harm. Perhaps a speedy treatment of Amnon after his rape of Tamar would have prevented the murder; perhaps a speedy reconciliation with Absalom would have healed that relationship. But David consistently used his power to isolate and to multiply pain.

Joab, David's general, saw the problem and knew that something had to be done, so he devised a ruse. Like father, like son,

---

[5]This is comparable to Dinah's dilemma (chapter 5); she could marry her rapist or go without marriage, and she may well have resented her brothers for making that choice for her.

[6]Absalom named one of his most beautiful daughters after Tamar (2 Samuel 14:27), but this seems a most meager compensation for a destitute life (2 Samuel 13:20).

like general.[7] Joab found a wise woman from the rural village of Tekoa, and brought her into the royal court. Joab tutored her on the things to say to David. She would pretend to be a rural widow seeking justice because one of her sons had killed the other. Now, her relatives wanted to kill the survivor for revenge, but that would leave the widow with no close kin at all. The wise woman presented her case, and David granted her justice (2 Samuel 14:1–11). Joab, as always, had done *too* good a job. The ruse was so clever that David gave the desired response, but he never saw himself in the picture. Joab's ruse succeeded so well that it failed.

The Tekoite woman then took the matter into her own hands. She condemned the king for his own life's actions, claiming that David's actions endangered everyone. As she phrased it, "For certainly we die, even like water poured on the ground, which cannot be gathered. If God does not direct one's desire, then God makes plans, lest one truly be banished from him" (2 Samuel 14:14). David's intransigence made death and dispersion inevitable, not just for David's family but for the nation as a whole. David removed God from his considerations, and so God was making other plans to try to save things.

This woman was capable of complex and nuanced theology, and she had the courage to speak this sharp critique directly to the king. She went beyond Joab's deceit and taught the king about Yahweh's intentions for him. Her courage and her wisdom gave her power, and her power healed the king, if only for a while. The Tekoite woman's power was not destructive power; it was restorative, positive power, used effectively (even in defiance of Joab's guidance) to improve the situation and to proclaim her faith in God.

Such wise women were the products of early Israel's rural life. Within each village, elders offered their leadership to the people. Wisdom passed down from one generation to the next, and those persons who lived long, observed their surroundings, and learned well the lessons of their elders soon gained a prominence that their ability to contribute in wisdom richly deserved. But the breakdown of rural life resulted in the diminishing of these sources of traditional wisdom and leadership. Instead, the monarchy centralized its decision-making, relying on the words of profes-

---

[7]Also, like prophet; Nathan's ruse announced the earlier problem with Bathsheba (2 Samuel 12:1–15).

sional advisers, such as the overzealous Joab and the cleverly deceitful Jonadab. When the monarchy centralized wisdom, it replaced local elders, both men and women, with male professionals.

The Tekoite woman offered a valuable contribution to the monarchy, but the monarchy was destroying the very process that had created her. She had her own agenda and the strength to carry it to its end, and the attempts to co-opt her into the monarchy's power structures failed. Soon, only men took such roles, and the king only listened to those on the royal payroll. Local traditions survived and so did local wisdom among both women and men, but the monarchy made sure that it was limited, when it managed to thrive at all.

A Place for Women

As the monarchy deepened its roots in Israel, it decreased the number of places for women. For this reason, we hear stories of the women in the royal family and the royal court, but not other women; slowly the monarchy crowded their voices into silence. No longer did as many women work in the fields; that was men's work. No longer did women rise to be wise elders and leaders; that work fell more and more to the professional men in the city.

Women had once shared the whole world with men, but increasingly the monarchy marginalized women. Soon, women's places were all inside, not in the fields, nor in the gates of the villages, nor even at the wells and marketplaces. We only hear of women within the palace itself. The monarchy had shrunk women's worlds into something much safer, much more manageable. Then, the real work of controlling and restricting women would begin.

Chapter **10**

Women
and the
Prophets

Prophecy is a term that covers a wide variety of phenomena. In modern times, *prophecy* usually refers to the act of predicting the future. Prophets tell their predictions in the grocery store checkout line scandal sheets, "prophesying" which celebrities will be pregnant next year and which will quit which television shows. Such prophecies are not worth the paper upon which they are printed.

Many churches throughout this country believe in some current manifestation of legitimate prophecy within the church. Usually, this prophecy occurs when the Holy Spirit invades an individual, producing an ecstatic effect that results in the uncontrollable utterance of a prediction about the future, often something that deals with the future of the church as a whole, a local congregation, or a member of that congregation. Prophecy, in this practice, becomes a partner to prayer. In prayer and praise, an individual speaks to God, and through prophecy, God speaks back, offering a contemporary and authoritative word for the present community of faith.

Prophecy in ancient Israel appeared in several different forms.[1] Especially in the years of early Israel's existence, ecstatic proph-

---

[1]For an overview of these forms and their historical development, as well as an introduction to each prophet, see Joseph Blenkinsopp, *A History of Prophecy in Israel from the Settlement in the Land to the Hellenistic Period* (Philadelphia: Westminster Press, 1983). For a more general introduction, see James M. Ward, *Thus Says the Lord: The Message of the Prophets* (Nashville: Abingdon Press, 1991).

119

ecy was somewhat frequent. These prophets danced and twirled until they felt possessed by Yahweh in a remarkable religious experience that showed Yahweh's true favor for the prophet (1 Samuel 10:10–13), but these ecstatic prophets never recorded utterances that they produced during these emotionally-charged moments.

A second type of prophet served within the royal court and delivered specific messages from God to the king. These prophets were parallel to secular advisers to government officials in modern times. They analyzed past and present situations to see what types of activities God blessed, and then made recommendations to kings and others about what to do next. Thus, prophets told David that adultery with Bathsheba was a sin and that punishment would come (2 Samuel 12:1–15), but prophets also told David that it was not the right time to build a temple (2 Samuel 7:2). Other prophets advised other kings about proper timing in starting military campaigns (1 Samuel 22:5; 1 Kings 22:5–12). Perhaps these court prophets specialized in their tasks, some focusing on internal politics, others on warfare policy, and so forth.[2] These prophets may have developed from local seers who could be hired to provide specific advice (1 Samuel 9:3–14; 10:2).

One group of prophets uttered statements that they wrote down themselves or that their followers recorded for posterity. These are the prophets best known from the Old Testament, such as Isaiah, Jeremiah, Hosea, and Amos. Because they produced statements that became written, they have books named after them in our canonical Old Testament, so their thoughts are more familiar to us. These prophets are theologians and social commentators. Unlike the first category of prophets, there is little evidence of ecstatic instances where God overtook their bodies to provide messages. They did provide political information like the second group, but they were much more interested in the reasons for God's action in the world than in specific advice about situations on the king's mind.

These prophets observed the status of their society and thought about their present, and then they offered a commentary on their contemporary situation that was based on the foundations of the ancient traditions of God's care and provision for the people. In this process of social commentary on the present, they also made some statements about the future, but this was not their focus;

---

[2]The woman Huldah seems to be this kind of prophet (2 Kings 22:14).

they wanted to show how the present situations would turn out if the people did not change their ways to match the will of God. These prophets were interpreters of the religious traditions in ways that demonstrated their relevance for the contemporary times.

In order to accomplish this mission, the prophets were forceful speakers. They were proficient poets and preachers who tried hard to persuade their audiences. This meant that they used shocking, surprising language to communicate their thoughts. Some of these metaphors and images went beyond the shocking to the truly disturbing. Prophets frequently used exaggeration in their attempts to gain the people's attention and to arouse them to the realities surrounding them. Prophets were highly critical observers of their social situations, so we should expect some very harsh attacks on the leaders of their day.

Critiques of Powerful Women

Some of these harsh attacks focused on women as members of the upper class. In these attacks, the prophets did not condemn power *per se,* but the decadence that comes from the poor use of power for selfish goals.

As the monarchy developed, the difference between the rich and the poor grew. Poor women in rural areas still labored in the fields and worked themselves to early deaths. Rich women, however, enjoyed a very different existence. They never worked outside their homes, where they had servants to take care of the domestic chores. Aside from pregnancy and childbirth, they had nothing to do. These rich women who lived in the cities formed a leisure class of persons who did not contribute to their society, but who lived off the labor and oppression of others. The prophets criticized these women fiercely.

Amos called these women "cows...who oppress the poor and break the needy, who say to their husbands, 'Bring me something, and let's drink!'" (Amos 4:1). These women relaxed in their wealth, never thinking that their leisure caused pain and suffering for others. Instead, they sat around in fancy houses so that they could drink themselves into oblivion all day long. They wanted their husbands to sit and drink with them, and their husbands could, because neither of them needed to labor in the fields or manage a business in order to survive.

Though Amos was extremely critical of these women, he did not seem to complain about them *because* they were women;

rather the great wealth in the face of the people's poverty angered the prophet. Thus, Amos also criticized both men and women whose wealth was so great.

> Woe to those who relax in Zion,
>> who are full of confidence in Mount Samaria,
> the noted ones of the chief of the nations,
>> to whom the house of Israel comes!
>
> Woe to those who rest on ivory beds,
>> and stretch themselves out on their couches,
> who eat the lambs from the flock,
>> and calves from the stall,
> who play around with the sound of the harp,
>> who like David compose for themselves on musical
>>> instruments,
> who drink from bowls of wine,
>> who anoint themselves with finest oil,
> but who do not care about the destruction of Joseph!
>> Amos 6:1, 4–6

Amos condemned all the rich who wasted their days lying in luxury, whether they were men or women. Amos' comments about the cows in Amos 4 were not denigrations of women, but denunciations of wealth and its excesses, especially when combined with complacency about the situation of other people.

Isaiah had similar concerns about wealth in general and wealthy women in particular in eighth-century Jerusalem. After an oracle that condemned the wealthy and powerful for grinding the faces of the poor into the ground, Isaiah tackled the problem of the wealthy women.

> Yahweh says:
> "Because the daughters of Zion have become arrogant,
>> because they walk with outstretched necks
>>> and seductive eyes,
>> walking and skipping and jingling their feet,
> the Lord will put scabs on the heads of Zion's daughters,
>> and Yahweh will open up their private parts.[3]
>>> Isaiah 3:16–17

---

[3]The Hebrew term here rendered "private parts" is much more graphic, and quite possibly obscene in the minds of original hearers of this prophecy. It is related to a term for "honeycomb."

Isaiah attacked the ostentatious displays of wealth by women who cared more for their finery than for the well-being of the people. In similar terms, Isaiah condemned the men of Jerusalem who had grown attached to their wealth and who thought they could never lose it. Isaiah tried to convince the wealthy people that they too were endangered by the same forces that threatened the poor. When foreign armies marched on Israel and Jerusalem to conquer them, all the money of the rich would not be enough to save them, so their concern should start right away with the prevention of strife. Isaiah argued with the people to forget their wealth and to remember their humanity.

These references to women in the prophets are extremely limited in scope. They deal with the wealthy women and decry their wealth, just as men's wealth and power receive condemnation. But other references in the prophets more directly discuss or assume the nature and status of women, and those texts will be much more difficult for us to read.

Gomer and Hosea

Hosea was one of the prophets active in Israel at roughly the same time and circumstances as Amos and Isaiah. In general, Hosea was more concerned about Israel's worship practices than Amos or Isaiah. Of course, all of these prophets spoke about worship, religion, politics, social practices, and other concerns in ways that were multifaceted and complex.

The Metaphor of Gomer

The book of Hosea begins with an extended metaphor in several stages. This prophet compared the people of Israel to a woman that Hosea was commanded to marry. Because this woman, Gomer, was unfaithful, God and Hosea rejected her, but in the end there is chance for restoration of relationship, though it is not clear if it is with Gomer or with another woman. The metaphor is a vicious, painful one.[4]

---

[4]For resources for the Gomer story, see Renita J. Weems, "Gomer: Victim of Violence or Victim of Metaphor?" *Semeia* 47 (1989): 87–104; and Fokkelien van Dijk-Hemmes, "The Imagination of Power and the Power of Imagination: An Intertextual Analysis of Two Biblical Love Songs: The Song of Songs and Hosea 2," *Journal for the Study of the Old Testament* 44 (1989) : 75–88.

The pain of the prophecy began with the characterization of Gomer. The prophet called her a prostitute, claiming that God sent him to marry a prostitute.[5] This formed the ground for the development of the metaphor. The text considered this woman dirty, soiled, and morally bankrupt, so the reader expects the relationship to fall apart. Furthermore, the reader expects to blame every failure on the woman. She was wicked, and she would be the one to cause the problems that were about to occur.

The prophet and his wife produced three children, and each received a negative name. *Jezreel* would be the place of Israel's death; *Lo-ruhamah* meant "no pity;" and *Lo-ammi* meant "not my people" (Hosea 1:6–9). These children, as well as their mother, represented Israel's unfaithfulness, and thus they prophesied Israel's coming destruction and abandonment. Then, Hosea's prophecy focused on the fate awaiting Gomer. Because she sought other lovers, Hosea demanded that she abandon her unfaithfulness or suffer punishment. This punishment would include death by exposure to the elements, being stripped naked in public and abandoned to die (Hosea 2:3). The treatment of Gomer was like Israel's loyalty to other gods, seeking from them instead of from Yahweh the means of life. Hosea would let Gomer starve, bereft of any comfort or means of life. There is also imagery of sexual violence (Hosea 2:10); the woman is the object of abuse and public humiliation.

Finally, Hosea allured Gomer back to him, as God would seduce Israel to return (Hosea 2:14—3:5). The punished woman would return sheepishly to the abusive husband, and then life would return to normal. All would be fine, and the horrors of the past could be forgotten. At least, it seemed that way to Hosea.

The Acceptance of Sexual Violence

In Hosea 1—3, the prophet marries Gomer and then threatens her with severe sexual violence. Not only does God support and command this atrocity, God also chooses sexual violence as a metaphor for how God relates to God's own people. Defense of this metaphorical choice is impossible.

---

[5] For understandings of prostitution in the Old Testament, see Phyllis Bird, "The Harlot as Heroine: Narrative Art and Social Presupposition in Three Old Testament Texts," *Semeia* 46 (1989): 119–139; and "'To Play the Harlot': An Inquiry into an Old Testament Metaphor," in *Gender and Difference in Ancient Israel,* ed. Peggy L. Day (Minneapolis: Fortress Press, 1989): 75–94.

In the ancient world, sexual and physical abuse were frequent events that possessed a certain social acceptance. No man would wish a reputation as a wife-beater or such, but as long as things did not become too public, probably not much was ever said. Public denunciations of abuse could continue, though most people would think them irrelevant, not realizing how widespread the problems really were. In other words, the ancient situation may not have been too different from our modern reality.

Hosea's metaphor built upon the partial public acceptance of sexual violence. The male audience would know of the situation and would accept it as appropriate behavior for a husband toward a disobedient wife. Perhaps there would be shock about the extent to which Hosea and Yahweh would go to punish the errant wife, but the acts themselves would not have surprised the audience as much as we wish that they would have.

The metaphor works today only insofar as we are willing to accept the assumptions behind it, chiefly the assumption of the appropriateness of sexual violence. When we reject that assumption, Hosea 1—3 seems sick and vile. Furthermore, this text seems to teach about God in ways we do not want to think. God is the violent, abusive one, approving of the horrible mistreatment of women. God's dominance becomes the important theological point, and God's ability to enforce that in ways of unspeakable pain becomes the necessary corollary. Grace and mercy come only after violence in this explanation of God's nature. This view of God is extremely problematic.

The Direction of the Metaphor

In this metaphor, Hosea and Gomer are comparable to God and Israel.[6] That is, the audience, Israel, was like Gomer. But the audience consisted of men, and probably only men. They would have seen themselves as the constituency of Israel; when all the men assemble, they *are* Israel. Hosea told these men that they are just like women.[7] As women, they would be subject to Yahweh's wrath and displeasure, and also to unlimited violence

---

[6]For further development of the use of this metaphor in Hosea 1—3, see Mary Joan Winn Leith, "Verse and Reverse: The Transformation of the Woman, Israel, in Hosea 1—3," in *Gender and Difference in Ancient Israel,* ed. Peggy L. Day (Minneapolis: Fortress Press, 1989): 95–108.

[7]This contradiction would also be present in the New Testament metaphor of the church as the bride of Christ (Ephesians 5:23–24).

from God. These men's own acceptance of violence to women trapped them; if these men themselves were like women before Yahweh, then Yahweh must have had the clear right to mistreat them as God saw fit. There could be no mercy if God chose not to provide it.

The men of Israel were God's woman, and God offered them a choice in this prophecy: be faithful to me or I will abuse you to death. The prophecy ended with the positive tones of restoration, but the salvation of the people depended entirely upon their willingness to be faithful.

Hosea forced the men to think of themselves as if they were women, to place themselves in some of women's most painful situations. Yet Hosea affirmed through this metaphor the continuation of the notions of male's dominance and Yahweh's dominance. Even more, Hosea equated those two types of dominance and accepted the potential role of violence in each.

Oholah and Oholibah

The prophet Ezekiel came almost two hundred years after Hosea, but also prophesied about sexual violence against women as an image of God. The prophet expounded a complex allegory, in which the people were two prostitutes whom God abused and killed because of their deeds (Ezekiel 23).[8]

The first woman was Oholah; she was compared to the Northern Kingdom of Israel. God had met Oholah and married her, but then Oholah lusted after others and sought other gods, so Yahweh gave her over to them. The Assyrians, a particularly vicious nation, killed her, with Yahweh's permission and approval, and so Oholah became known posthumously throughout the world as an example of what can happen to a woman who goes wrong.

God had also loved and married Oholah's younger sister, Oholibah, who represented Jerusalem and the Southern Kingdom of Judah.[9] Oholibah was even more unfaithful than her sister, and Yahweh's punishment of her was correspondingly more severe. Yahweh arranged a gang rape to teach her a lesson. "Thus says Yahweh God: 'I am going to give you into the power of the men

---

[8]For a further development of Ezekiel 23, see Jon L. Berquist, *Ezekiel: Surprises by the River* (St. Louis: Chalice Press, forthcoming), ch. 6.

[9]The law of Leviticus 18:18 forbids sexual relations with two sisters, but Ezekiel shows no recognition of this probably later law.

you hate, into the power of the men who repulse you. They will treat you with hatred, and will take away everything you have worked for. They will leave you naked and vulnerable; they will uncover the genitals with which you were unfaithful'" (Ezekiel 23:28–29). God also forced Oholibah to watch the execution of her own children (Ezekiel 23:25, 47). Abuse runs rampant through this text.

For Ezekiel, this extended metaphor functioned as an explanation of exile. Because Israel had worshiped other gods, they deserved punishment, and God's chosen form of chastisement was exile, the forced removal of the Israelites from their land. This also involved the Babylonian army's slaughter of thousands of Israelites. Ezekiel equated this pain and loss with the injury, suffering, and humiliation of gang rape.

Behind the metaphor lies assumptions, once more. For Ezekiel, the assumption is that things happen for reasons. In other words, bad things happen to the people who deserve them. Bad things never happen to good people; only the evil suffer. Exile came to Israel because they sinned. Without arguing Ezekiel's theological point, the metaphor that he used to communicate this idea would work if and only if the same was true about women victimized by sexual violence. For the metaphor to succeed, the audience must assume that rape victims deserve what happens to them, and victims of gang rape deserve it even more.

If Ezekiel and his audience would have thought of rape as random, pointless violence, then this extended metaphor would have meant that Israel did not deserve what happened to it, but that God could not control such things. Some good nations were exiled, and some bad nations were, and that is just that. But Ezekiel was making the opposite point: Israel deserved its punishment, and God desired their abasement. Ezekiel must have thought the same thing about rape.

Our communities of faith must be very hesitant about the use of texts such as Hosea 1—3 and Ezekiel 23. These prophetic denunciations intended to condemn the men of Israel for their failure to stay faithful and loyal to Yahweh, and we have no reason to minimize this religious concern. People today need reminders of the importance of faithfulness to God, just as the ancients did. But the words *do* get in the way. These metaphors not only teach the point of loyalty, but they also communicate certain assumptions that are extremely dangerous. Since the metaphors assume that husbands can abuse wives to maintain discipline and that rape victims deserve that atrocity, we will never hear the prophets' point unless we also accept the assumptions. That price is too high, far too high; there are other ways to make the point of loyalty without demeaning women. Instead, modern communities of faith must together insist that faith's desire is the end of abuse, even though our own history contains too much of it.

Prophets and the Abuse of Women

The deeper problem within these texts is the description of God with images of male violence and male dominance. Some argue that the image of God as spouse-abuser was just the application of an available metaphor, a piece of common experience that could lead to the communication of an important, though painful, point. But the situation is not that neutral. Truly, these prophets *intended* their message to shock; they violate the ancient sense of common decency by going much, much too far, just as they do with modern sensitivities. Prophets often violate norms for communicative effect; in that sense, this case is no different.

Even in the face of their other uses of language, these prophets advocate the continuation of such structures and expectations of oppression and violence of women, simply through their construction of metaphors that depend upon such assumptions. Our communities of faith cannot afford to continue to spread these assumptions, or to render divine support for such utter evil, even inadvertently.

These texts are among the most difficult in the Bible for theological reflection. Certainly, we can (and must) begin by saying that these are antiquated human views of God; they are not God's own self-understanding. Thus, we can stand at a distance and critique the societies that claim divine support for abuse of women. But the problem goes deeper, because these stories are based on the thought that God punishes for sin and that people deserve such punishment.

The Problem with Sacrifice

Because this thinking is so much a part of modern Christian faith, our own critique must go further.[10] God the powerful pun-

---

[10]For much more complete attempts to deal with this immense problem, see Rita Nakashima Brock, *Journeys by Heart: A Christology of Erotic*

isher has not proved to be a sufficient image for God. To the contrary, this image has legitimated power and punishment, such as abuse, throughout the last two thousand years. Worship of a God of Power has tempted us over and over again to attain power and then to use it. Too often, we have concentrated on the types of destructive power that are often associated with men in the Bible. Certainly, in these prophetic metaphors, God's power is destructive; it is the power to kill and to injure, to abuse and to demean. This is not the power of God to save. It would be extremely difficult to see any of God in such ultimate destructive power, except for our long-standing theological traditions, including these prophecies.

The concept of sacrifice, especially Jesus' sacrifice, has shaped Christianity to a great extent. Sacrificial thinking is very problematic, to say the least. One traditional formulation of Christianity is that we are supposed to believe in a kind and loving God *because* God painfully killed the divine Christ because of anger at other people's sins. Because God's wrath required a *victim*, God's own Son went to death, even the painful, humiliating death on a cross. Sacrifices require victims; there is no other way to have a sacrifice. A religion based on sacrifices will continue to purport victimization. When Jesus is the sacrifice, then we have a God who supports and encourages the victimization of the innocent as a holy act. To endure suffering is to be like Jesus, and that encourages suffering and pain. Such hardly seems the intention of God's gift of Christ; it cannot be grace.

The problem of sacrificial thought has long been recognized in Christianity, even though we rarely act upon our knowledge. Sacrifice means that we save ourselves. God has given us a mechanism by which to do it, but the sacrifice is what we do. Modern Christian appropriation of this often emphasizes that we "accept" Christ's sacrifice, but that still means that we do the final act of salvation ourselves. When we "give up" dependence on self, we are still making a sacrifice that allows us to save ourselves. Sacrifice still requires a victim, and in Christianity, the prototypical victim is human and divine, not merely an animal as in early Israelite worship.

Power (New York: Crossroad, 1988); and Joanne Carlson Brown and Carole R. Bohn, eds., *Christianity, Patriarchy, and Abuse: A Feminist Critique* (New York: Pilgrim Press, 1989).

Perhaps a hint toward a way out of this problem can come from the two confessions of sin in Hosea. The first of these confessions has a haunting beauty.

> "Come, let us return to Yahweh.
> It is God who has torn us;
>> God will heal us.
> God struck;
>> God will bandage us.
> God will make us live after two days;
>> on the third day, God will raise us,
>>> and we will live in God's presence.
> Let us know,
>> let us pursue the knowing of Yahweh.
> God's coming is as certain as dawn;
>> God will come like rain to us,
>>> like the showers that moisten the earth."
>>>> Hosea 6:1–3

This confession sounds much like standard, traditional Christian faith. God will take care of us and will give us life. When we make this confession of faith and return to God, then God's coming is certain. There is sacrificial thought; when we do this, we have God under control. Once we meet God's requirements, then God *must* save us. God has no choice. We do the thing that saves and then God has no choice but to save. Thus, it should not surprise us that God rejects this confession (Hosea 6:4–6). What is God's reason? "I prefer loyalty rather than sacrifices, knowing God rather than burnt offerings" (Hosea 6:6).

But there is another confession in the book of Hosea.

> "Return, O Israel, unto Yahweh your God,
>> because you have stumbled in your sin.
> Take with you words;
>> return to Yahweh;
> Say to God,
>> 'Remove all sin;
>> take what is good;
>> let us offer the fruit of our lips.'
> Assyria can't save us;
>> we will not ride upon horses.

> We will never again say 'Our God!' to the work of our
> hands,
> because we orphans find mercy in you."
>
> Hosea 14:1–3

God accepts this confession and heals the people. God changes them inside and removes their sin and their disloyalty (Hosea 14:4). God wants to save us, but first we must realize that we do not save ourselves, either through sacrifice or through anyone else's sacrifice. God saves. God wants the loyalty that comes after salvation. In any sacrificial system, the human action precedes the divine response that gives favor or salvation, but in God's desire, God saves and then people respond. This is truly radical grace from a God whose love overwhelms any of us.

Punishment has little role in this view of God's reality. If God punishes us for our bad deeds and rewards us for our good ones (such as faith), then there is sacrifice and there are victims. Humans cannot save themselves, even and especially through victimization. Hosea 1—3 and Ezekiel 23 still believe that people deserve punishment, but Hosea 6 and 14 already contain the seeds, probably unrealized by the prophet, of a new way of thinking about God. In this new way, there are no deserving victims and there is no punishing God who demands sacrifices and sacrificial victims. It is not this kind of sacrifice that God desires, it is loyalty and faithfulness. God desires the intimacy that can come only when the fear of abuse is absent. This means that today's communities of faith must work toward a world where intimacy is possible and abuse is absent, for women and for all.

Chapter **11**

Lady
Wisdom

Israel's monarchy produced many changes within Israelite society. One of these changes was the creation of a group of professional scribes. Royal administration required written records, and so the kings assembled a group of people who could write in order to maintain those records, write contracts, send letters to the outreaches of the empire and to different nations, and to accumulate the wisdom of the nation. These scribes also taught writing to the next generation of scribes, and this reality helped to produce a tightly-knit group identity among these government servants. The scribes formed a separate guild within Israel, and they were powerful because they controlled a very precious resource within the nation. The ability to write was rare, so these scribes gained influence from their ability to do what few others could.

Over the years, the scribes developed a tradition of recording and compiling wisdom. Such wisdom includes proverbs and other short statements about life's reality, as well as longer pieces of philosophy and speculative thought. Wisdom books within the Old Testament canon include Proverbs, Ecclesiastes, Job, and the Song of Songs. Within the apocryphal or deuterocanonical books, which are accepted by Catholic, Ortho- dox, and certain other traditions, there are additional books, such as the Book of Wisdom and Sirach. Scribes wrote and rewrote these compilations of wise thoughts, keeping alive this tradition of thinking about the world.[1]

Of course, the scribes in Jerusalem were not the only people in Israel thinking about the world in these ways. Local communities were important sources of wisdom. Village elders and others developed quips about the way life really is, and they passed these short sayings down to their children. In this fashion, many important proverbs existed for generations without any written record. In Jerusalem, the king's scribes may have written down some of these rural proverbs, as they had chance to hear of them.

Many of the recorded wisdom sayings in the Old Testament deal with the nature and status of women. Also, both wisdom and folly are described as if they were women, and so this provides a further basis for investigating these scribes' understandings of women.

The Nature of Women

The proverbs of Israel's scribes were taught by men to men, and so they deal with women from a male perspective. Proverbs do not tell women what to do and how to live; proverbs tell *men* what to think and do *about* women. Primarily, this takes the form of advice about wives. A good wife is extremely valuable. "A strong woman is the crown of her husband" (Proverbs 12:4). Perhaps it would be more accurate to say that a good wife is a wonderful *thing* for a man to have; women are often possessions in the wisdom thought. Because of the male perspective in the tradition, there is no comment that women's virtue is positive in and of itself, but only that a woman's moral strength benefits her husband. Nevertheless, this proverb does offer a positive statement about women within the limitations of that context. Women's virtue is affirmed as valuable.

The proverbs also encourage men to think of women in terms of inner strength rather than outer beauty. "Like a gold ring in the nose of a wild boar is a beautiful woman who lacks perception" (Proverbs 11:22). Perception, or perhaps intellect or taste, is

---

[1]For general introduction to the wisdom literature of the Old Testament, see James L. Crenshaw, *Old Testament Wisdom: An Introduction* (Atlanta: John Knox Press, 1981); and Roland E. Murphy, *The Tree of Life: An Exploration of Biblical Wisdom Literature* (Anchor Bible Reference Library; Garden City, New York: Doubleday, 1991).

more important than the physical attributes of loveliness. This is an important point for the status of women, because it evaluates women on the same scale as men. Inner qualities determine an individual's worth, not any outer manifestations. Attractiveness is an unimportant facet in this view, but both men and women need sense and insight. The life of the mind then opens not only for these men who work as scribes and who accumulate the wisdom of the ages, but also for women, who should show evidence of intellect and perception.

The reverse is also true for these proverbs. Nagging, bickering women receive harsh condemnation. "Staying in a corner of the rooftop is better than a quarrelsome wife and a house in strife" (Proverbs 25:24). "A leaky roof with a steady drip on a day of downpours and a quarrelsome wife are just the same; sheltering her is sheltering wind" (Proverbs 27:15–16). These proverbs play upon stereotypical images of women as quarreling, quibbling creatures who squabble over insignificant items.

Our culture might rephrase one of these proverbs as, "Leaky roofs deserve to be plugged up, and so does the mouth of a bickering woman." If you can't ignore the noise, make it go away. Shut it up. There is no sense in these that women might be right, or that men might be oversensitive to women's criticism. Instead, there is the continuing assumption that women do not know of what they speak and should not bother men with such things. Men think about real things, things of weight and substance, but women's minds are flighty, focusing only on the frivolous things best left unheard.

Though the proverbs do emphasize the value of women as thinking, perceptive persons, they also reinforce the stereotypes about women that demean and limit women. These bits of wisdom encourage men to think highly of women, but still to think of women within the traditional structure of that society's thought.

The Stranger

Old, traditional structures of thought dominate Proverbs, often perpetuating stereotypes of all sorts. One of these preconceived and fixed images is that of the woman of the streets, who seduces thinkers into her evil sway.

This evil woman appears frequently throughout the book of Proverbs. This image operates on two levels. First, the sayings remind men to avoid sexual relationships with women other than their wives. Second, the sayings emphasize the importance of faithfulness to the one way of thinking presented in the sayings themselves; loyalty to no other teachings is permitted.[2] This is especially clear in the early chapters of the book of Proverbs, where the double meaning becomes apparent.

> The lips of a strange woman drip sweet honey;
> > her palate is as slippery as oil.
> In the end, she tastes bitter, like wormwood;
> > sharp, like a two-edged sword.
> Her feet go down to death;
> > her steps sink down to Sheol.
>
> Proverbs 5:3–4

This "strange woman" provides sexual attraction, but men who pursue and fulfill that seduction follow this woman straight to hell. Likewise, the discourse of nongodly voices within the world attracts the scribes' attention, but following those other voices (whether religious, philosophical, ethical, or other) leads only to death. Only the wisdom of Yahweh, as preserved in books like Proverbs, leads to life.

This woman is "strange" in a specific sense: she is not the man's wife. Thus, this woman is outside the system within which the scribes understand their universe. To go to the woman or to pursue her would be to step outside the system and thus to violate the universal order that the scribes value so greatly. Perhaps the woman is ethnically or geopolitically foreign, but that is not necessary; she could be a faithful Israelite just as well. The danger can come from without and from within; neither direction is absolutely safe.

The sin of adultery receives special attention, because adultery broke the order of one man faithfully married to one faithful woman, an order that protected men's property rights as well. An adulterous woman threatens a man's life (Proverbs 6:26; 30:20), and just like burning coals, adultery is playing with fire (Proverbs 6:28). Adulterers are deadly snares (Proverbs 7:23); they are pits to trap the unwary (Proverbs 22:14; 23:27).

In short, the book of Proverbs understands the whole universe to contain a cosmic order. Humans violate that universal order

---

[2]Cp. Carol A. Newsom, "Woman and the Discourse of Patriarchal Wisdom: A Study of Proverbs 1—9," in *Gender and Difference in Ancient Israel,* ed. Peggy L. Day (Minneapolis: Fortress Press, 1989), pp. 142–160.

only at grave risk to themselves and others. Sexual fidelity in marriage is part of that cosmic order, and so it should be maintained without exception. This means that women should be kept in their place—married to one man and loyal to him. This dependence on order and the settled nature of existence produced many of the moral codes still in effect.

The Ideal Woman

Not only does the book of Proverbs discuss strange women who represent dangers, the last lengthy proverb within the book emphasizes the correct role for women (Proverbs 31:10–31). Though this is a dangerous vision that has historically been used to limit women's roles, many women have found it comforting.

This poem begins with the rhetorical question, "Who can find a strong woman? She is far more valuable than jewels" (Proverbs 31:10). The subject of the poem is the ideal woman, which is the same for these scribes as the ideal wife. The key to this woman is that she benefits her husband in a myriad of ways. She works with textiles and fabrics (vs. 13, 19, 22, 24); she engages in profitable commerce (vs. 14, 16, 24); she exercises and strengthens herself (v. 17); she shows generosity to the needy (v. 20); she teaches wisdom and faith (vs. 26, 30). For this, she receives the admiration of her husband and her children alike (vs. 28–29), and perhaps even a share of the wealth that she herself has created (v. 31). She is the perfect wife, and she receives the due for her perfection.

Reactions to this poem's depiction of women vary widely. Does it restrict women or expand their possibilities? Does it limit their value or overwork them? Several possible evaluations of the whole poem are worthy of consideration.

A first reaction is praise. The poem deserves our recognition because of its positive depiction of women in a variety of tasks. This woman goes beyond the norms for her society by involving herself in many tasks that were considered primarily male, such as the buying and selling of land and the management of international commerce. Therefore, the poem asserts women's abilities to perform these social roles and their right to do so. This poem should encourage women because of the permission and support that it gives in trying various roles. It is a poem of liberation, opening up opportunities to women who might otherwise be denied these options.

A second reaction is opposition. This poem limits women's value as women. This so-called "perfect" woman never does anything for herself; she gains fame only because she makes a *man* rich and happy. She never receives the credit for her awesome labors; it all goes to her husband. Further, she does the work typically expected of her husband, and he seems to do nothing except sit at the gate and talk with his friends. By this reading, this poem is male fantasy about the perfect wife, who does all of his work for him and still adores him enough to wait on him hand and foot. At the end of his day, she meets him at the door, wearing something slinky, with a martini in one hand and his slippers in the other, and says, "Dinner will be on the table in fifteen minutes; it's your favorite. Do you want to read the paper first?" Such male fantasy demeans women, because it allows women no room to experience life as themselves, as women. Instead, all women's experiences center on care and aggrandizement of men.

A third response is that the poem asks too much from women. It fuels the superwoman myth. This woman wakes up early and has half-a-day's work done before anyone else wakes up, and then she stays up late finishing some extra projects. The perfect woman is a perfect wife, mother, homemaker, worker, model citizen, and everything else. She never stops, she never slows down, she never gets sick, and she never takes a vacation. The job never ends because it is far too much for any woman to ever do. If this poem's notion of perfection requires all that work, it's just impossible. And what's the use of an impossible model?

All of these reactions are valid. Perhaps the poem reaches its greatest usefulness if conceived as a list of options and possibilities. Certainly, all of these roles are appropriate ones for women, but must the list stop there? If this wide of a range of activities are allowed for women, perhaps others can be added. Wisdom is an accumulative process, and so this would fit quite well. Also, the question of motive can be addressed. Must women perform these tasks for men, or can the same tasks be performed for their intrinsic rewards as well? If so, then it proves possible to expand this list to include the things that women can do for self-sufficiency and self-respect. Within this interpretation, the list of Proverbs 31:10–31 may be able to energize women's self-determination and actualizing activity, without limiting roles, subordinating women to men, or overworking women.

It is striking how little importance this poem gives to childbirth. Though this woman appears to be a mother of grown children, her productivity that enlivens her husband is not procreation. Childbirth, which had become the only real contribution for women early in the monarchy, here loses its centrality and becomes a merely peripheral event in this woman's life. Of course, whether this marginalizing of childbearing is liberating of or disconfirming to women's experience is open to debate.

Lady Wisdom

When the scribes responsible for the biblical collection of Proverbs compiled them, there was special attention to the strange, unknown woman on the street, who might call to the unwary male passer-by with offers of adultery, prostitution, or even unfamiliar and unapproved wisdom discourse. This figure of the strange woman loomed larger than life, casting dark shadows that threatened the continuation of fidelity and wisdom. But these scribes preserved for later generations the figure of another larger-than-life woman, as well. Her name is Wisdom.[3]

Wisdom stands at the crossroads, in the public square, in the very heights of the town and makes her call for fidelity and devotion (Proverbs 8:1–3; 9:1–6). From this vantage point, all the males of the community can come forward and receive instruction from this Lady Wisdom. This woman speaks forth noble truths (8:6–9). She controls the counsel of the nations, by which means she directs the outcomes of international politics (8:14–16). Her benefits are numerous for her devotees.

> I love those who love me;
> > those who intently seek me will find me.
> Wealth and glory are mine;
> > permanent sufficiency and righteousness.
> My fruit is better than gold, better than fine gold,
> > and my results are better than choice silver.
> I walk in ways of righteousness,
> > amidst the paths of justice,
> > so that I can give an inheritance to those

---

[3]For an examination of the use of Lady Wisdom in liturgy, see Susan Cady, Marian Ronan, and Hal Taussig, *Wisdom's Feast: Sophia in Study and Celebration* (San Francisco: Harper and Row, 1990).

> who love me.
> Certainly, even their treasuries will I fill.
>> Proverbs 8:17–20

Lady Wisdom gives all these benefits to those who follow her, walking in the paths of wisdom.[4] These routes are also the paths of justice and righteousness, uniting these images of a supernatural woman named Wisdom with the highest ideals of Israel's prophets. Usually, Israel's scribes discussed wisdom as a way to gain wealth for one's self, whereas Israel's prophets talked about the need to share prosperity among the people. Lady Wisdom combines these notions and asserts that she answers both sets of expectations. She is peace and wholeness in a world where such things are rare.

Lady Wisdom shared the tasks of creation with Lord Yahweh. Together, they made everything that is seen and experienced by humanity. Lady Wisdom was the first of Yahweh's creations (8:22–29). The Lady's task was that of building; she was the Lord's chief artisan in the creation of the world (8:30). She was with God from the beginning, and through her were all things created. Lady Wisdom rejoiced in the creation of the world and its inhabitants; she celebrated humanity with dancing (8:31). Then, the Lady set up a banquet on earth for all the world's peoples to come and join with her around that grand table of community (9:1–6). Lady Wisdom provides instruction to all the peoples, and that instruction is the first step toward knowing God (8:13; 9:6). She is the path through whom all come to know God, and apart from her there is no other way.[5]

These images show us Lady Wisdom in a very similar way to how the New Testament later portrayed Jesus Christ. Lady Wisdom, though a creation of God, is a divine being in Proverbs 8—9. She worked with God in the creation of all other things; she was in the beginning, and she was with God, and she cocreated with God. Then, in Proverbs 9, she arrives on the earth as the incarnation of God, the one true path to reach Yahweh. These are powerful images. Most strikingly, they are female images. Here is a deity in metaphor, who is accessible to the people rather than

---

[4]As other depictions of women in this culture, Lady Wisdom gives of herself for others' benefit—especially the benefit of men.

[5]The New Testament has developed most of these images to describe Jesus' role in creation and in table fellowship.

existing far away as Yahweh too often did, and this figure is female!

Lady Wisdom did not violate later Israel's staunch monotheism. However, she did provide a female manifestation of the deity. She was not God, and she was not a goddess, but she was extremely close to Yahweh God, to the extent that she was Yahweh's partner. Though worship of Lady Wisdom would be a contravention of monotheism, the recognition and respect for Lady Wisdom would not be objectionable at all. The people of Israel, both women and men, could rejoice in this powerful image of God in female terms, and could use this image as a way to understand and approach God through female terms and concepts.

Another intriguing female figure in the wisdom literature is the woman in the explicit love poetry called the Song of Songs. This woman is an open, erotic lover. She embodies a fresh acceptance of life in all its possibilities and enjoyment. She integrates body and spirit into one core of life.

In this, the woman lover in the Song teaches us about Wisdom. Wisdom is accessible, open, and willing. Wisdom enjoys life and dances in celebration at life's wondrous possibilities. Wisdom makes the potential real, by appearing in ways that attract others to experience the life of wisdom and its ways. Faithfulness underlies the character of both the woman in the Song of Songs and Lady Wisdom in Proverbs. Both are oriented toward another in relationships of complete fidelity, one to a male lover and the other to Yahweh God. Both know the other in intimate ways. Both are vibrantly female and voraciously alive in their self-determination. They both integrate identity and intimacy.

For humans, Lady Wisdom becomes a channel to God. Wisdom's faithfulness to Yahweh is a beacon to us for us to follow. Her intimacy with our creator provides the model for our intimacy with God. Yet Lady Wisdom also offers the example of motivated love that springs from a deep sense of identity and independence. She approaches God in intimacy because she is her own self, as she was created to be. Likewise, God created us in Yahweh's image, but with capacities for independence that could lead to intimate relations and capacities for intimacy that could lead to independent self-awareness. This proves a powerful image for women to use in development of their own spiritual intimacy with God.

Chapter 12

Ruth

Few of the Bible's stories about women are as memorable as Ruth's tale. Perhaps this is just as it should be, since this is one of the most positive portrayals of women in the Old Testament. Also, the story is important because it offers at least three intriguing examples of women in Ruth, Naomi, and the women of their community. All of this appears in a deceptively simple narrative with characters that capture the imagination, combining to form a story that has impacted communities of faith for millennia.

The narrative's brevity deceives us into thinking that it is simple. There is hardly any attribution of motive throughout the story; the narrator rarely tells us *why* things happen. This provides us, the story's modern readers, with amazing latitude as we struggle to determine why these characters perform as they do and what it all means. At first, it seems that the meaning is clear, but as soon as we try to focus on that meaning and to state it with precision, we start to find the difficulties.

Perhaps one of the story's most intriguing features is the very thing that makes it so difficult to understand. The book of Ruth presents a world that is very much a world of women. In most of the Old Testament stories there are no women present at all, and even when there are women, they are all too often silent. In the many stories where women play significant roles, still there is usually only one significant woman. Take, for instance, the story of Dinah (Genesis 34).[1] The story begins with a young woman,

---

[1] See above, chapter 5.

141

Dinah, who is described as the daughter of another woman, Leah (Genesis 34:1). As the story begins, there are only two women as the named characters. Dinah goes to visit the women of the land. The story starts as a story of a women's world. But the story fails immediately. Leah herself never appears, and all the rest of the characters are men. Dinah never speaks, and men determine her fate at every twist of the narrative's journey. Dinah is a woman trapped within a male world, where she can have no control over her own life. Such is the type of story we have come to expect from the majority of Old Testament stories about women.

The book of Ruth is quite different, however. There are multiple female characters who control their own lives, and they exercise that control throughout the story. The narrative's women interact with each other and make decisions together (or at least in relationship with each other). In the story's final scene (Ruth 4:14–17), both Ruth and Naomi seem to be present, surrounded by the local community of women. If Boaz is around at all, he is silently standing in a corner without any interaction. The only male who is undoubtedly present is the silent child, Obed, who does nothing. The women are in firm control of their own situations, and they interact together, while the men are almost entirely absent from the story's end.

This narrative presents its readers with a woman's world, and the Bible does that so rarely that we modern interpreters are taken unaware by this vision. We can hardly depend on our competence in reading the other biblical stories to help us very much in our study of Ruth, since these other stories are so different. How do we go about interpreting this women's world? We must wrestle with this question as we go through Ruth's story.

In Distant Moab

This tale begins in the city of Bethlehem, near Jerusalem, but it doesn't stay there for very long. Within the first verse, even before the characters have names, the family lives in Bethlehem and then moves away to the distant land of Moab. The family renounces its citizenship in Israel and becomes resident aliens in a foreign land, Moab.

The narrative gives only one reason for their move: there was famine. Hunger drove them out of their homeland. Because of the hunger, the family was willing to surrender its rights of citizenship. When the basic needs of life clamor loudly enough, people give up their basic rights and other benefits of legal abstraction in order to find things such as food and shelter. This is a family in true crisis, existing on the border of starvation. Perhaps they had once been wealthy or at least of adequate means, but those days had long since passed. Whatever they had once owned had been sold to pay for food, and now even that was gone. This family marched off into a new land with little to show for their time in Bethlehem. They were destitute and desperate.

The crisis grows to immense proportions. As if famine was not enough, death followed right on its heels, striking first Elimelech, Naomi's husband (Ruth 1:3). The next verse contains two subtler tragedies, but they add to the crisis nonetheless. Naomi's two sons, Machlon and Chilion, married Moabite wives. This was a tragedy, since it would dilute the purity of Naomi's grandchildren, and it would make any subsequent reintegration into Israelite life all the more difficult, since Moabites were not well accepted in Naomi's homeland. The next tragedy follows right behind, and the narrative barely mentions it at all. In fact, the reader only sees the tragedy because of what the narrative does *not* say. In order to follow typical Hebrew narrative style, the story should say that the boys took wives and then had sons. But the second half of that statement is missing; instead, the reader finds "they lived there ten years" (Ruth 1:4). Naomi's sons' marriages were unproductive and infertile; there were no offspring at all. The family was at its end, and this only added to the tragedy.

Then the crisis took its final step: Naomi's sons died. Suddenly, without any knowable reason, they died. At this point, the story states the crisis in its barest form: Naomi had no sons and no husband. This becomes the problem that the story strives to solve throughout the development of its plot. Naomi, who is a loyal faithful Israelite woman, must have a man. Husbands and sons are both allowed at first, but there must be a man to support Naomi. Her culture required a man for economic survival, and so she needed a man to save her. The crisis for Naomi *includes* all of these elements that leave her without a man, such as the famine that took her away from her extended kin, the death of her husband, the marriage of her sons to worthless foreigners, the infertility of those Moabite girls, and the death of her sons.

Even within the first chapter, the answer becomes clear—but the answer is clearly unbelievable.

Naomi begins the long trek home, back to Bethlehem, where there might be some kin to offer some solution to her. At first, both of her daughters-in-law wish to go with her, but Naomi discourages them. Life would be better for these young women if they would stay around Moab, where they were known. Though both of them were already proven infertile and may have caused the death of their husbands (at least, that's what the rumors would say, to be sure—it would be rare for anyone to have blamed the men for the lack of children), they would have a better chance of getting husbands in Moab than anywhere else. Naomi advises them to stay, and Orpah agrees. If everyone just goes back home, then perhaps everyone could pretend that the problems never existed. Ruth, on the other hand, wants to *solve* the problems. Ruth knows what the solution requires: Naomi must have a husband or a son (and preferably both), and so must Ruth. Naomi argues that she is too old to take a husband or to provide a son that could be a husband to Ruth or to anyone else.

For that matter, Naomi was right. She was being realistic; within the normal ways of life, there was no opportunity for her to find husband or son to take care of her. Ruth was just making Naomi restate the obvious facts that no one wanted to say aloud: Naomi didn't stand a chance. That's when Ruth proposed her own solution, which was more than a little unorthodox.

Ruth offered to marry Naomi. In the text's words, "Ruth clung to Naomi" (Ruth 1:14). This verb *cling* refers to the male role in initiating marriage.[2] Outside of the book of Ruth, this verb never refers to a woman's action. When Ruth clings to Naomi, Ruth takes the male role in initiating a relationship of formal commitment, similar to marriage.

Of course, this marriage would not be like any other, but still the point was clear. Ruth and Naomi would join their fates together and would travel together. They would worship the same God and even be buried together. Though this could not be a "real" marriage in the sense understood by ancient Israelite society, Ruth would manifest the loyalty of marriage and would work to solve Naomi's problem. If Ruth were a "real" husband to Naomi, then the "marriage" would have solved everything instantly. Instead, Ruth becomes a sort of surrogate husband. Ruth will play the part until a real husband comes along. Or Ruth will get a son for Naomi, and that son will solve the problem. Naomi's

---

[2]Cp. Genesis 34:3; Joshua 23:12; and 1 Kings 11:2.

solution depends upon a husband or a son; Ruth as surrogate husband would provide the son.

Ruth adds a new role. In order to solve Naomi's problem or even to work toward it in meaningful ways that bring progression to the narrative, Ruth must act in new ways. She must go beyond the old limits in which she acted. She does not leave her old roles behind her when this transformation comes; she is still Naomi's daughter-in-law, even though she now takes the role of a clinger. By adding roles, she responds to the crisis in ways that have the power to transform herself and her situation.[3] Naomi still sees herself in terms of her old roles: wife and mother. Because she can no longer fulfill those specific roles, she feels that life is over for her. Orpah leaves to sustain her old roles of Moabitess and wife. Only Ruth, at this early point in the story, is willing to add new roles, including that of Naomi's husband.

A Short-term Solution

Ruth knows that the crisis is severe and that it needs a quick remedy. However, the situation is very bleak, and it is not likely that a permanent solution can be found in a short length of time. So Ruth sets out looking for a short-term solution. Ruth desires some situation that can keep her and Naomi alive for a while, so that she can have time to work on a permanent solution. The problem has already been stated: Naomi needs either a husband (and Ruth won't do in the long run) or a son. But in the meantime, they both need to eat. That's the immediate priority.

For the immediate problem, Ruth finds a short-term solution: gleaning (Ruth 2:2). Ancient Israelite law required each farmer to leave small plots of land at the corners of each field unharvested, to allow needy persons to take that grain for themselves. Farmers should always exercise good stewardship, but not to the point where efficiency turns into greed. For these Israelites, that boundary line was at the corners of the fields. Also, these farmers should make sure that their hired help did not work so hard that

---

[3]The classic example of crisis-induced role addition is the women who took factory jobs in the United States during the Second World War. They added roles that went beyond their previous tasks and identities. In doing so, they transformed the crisis situation by providing previously impossible solutions, and they also transformed themselves, catalyzing a social change toward women in the workplace that is still going on today, nearly a half-century later.

they gathered every scrap of grain. If something fell to the ground, the workers should just let it stay there. This would allow needy people to come through the fields later and pick up the grain that remained. It would not be much, but it might make the difference between life and death for some. Landowners' right to profit ended sharply and permanently at the point where it might cost someone else life itself.[4]

Gleaning, therefore, provided a short-term solution to Ruth's problem of possible starvation. Even though gleaning was back-breaking work that would place Ruth in the midst of the worst elements in the society, she is willing to do what it takes to support her new-found family, Naomi. No labor is too hard. But gleaning could never be a long-term solution. As soon as the harvest season was over, there would be nothing left to glean. Though Ruth might be able to gather a bit more each day than she and Naomi would eat, it would be impossible to save up enough grain to last all winter long.

Ruth the Moabitess became Naomi's husband, and now she becomes gleaner as well. But she is also busy making other plans for her future.

A Long-term Solution

At the same time that Ruth begins her short-term solution of gleaning, she also sets in motion a long-term solution. She will get Naomi a son, and that means that Ruth must get herself a husband, and preferably a well-to-do husband who can afford to care for Ruth and for Naomi from the start. When Ruth sets out in her new role as gleaner, she seeks another role at the same time: seductress.

Again, most English translations miss the point. When Ruth announces her intentions to glean, she says, "I intend to go to the field, so that I may glean among the grain after anyone *in whose eyes I find favor*" (Ruth 2:2). Usually, interpreters treat this as Ruth's search for someone kind who would allow her to glean. Certainly this expression can be used to indicate an asking for permission. But Ruth does *not* need to ask permission in order to

---

[4]For the Old Testament's gleaning laws, see Leviticus 19:9–10; 23:22; Deuteronomy 24:18–22. See also Jon L. Berquist, *Ancient Wine, New Wineskins: The Lord's Supper in Old Testament Perspective* (St. Louis: Chalice Press, 1991), pp. 90–91.

glean in anyone's field; the law gives her the inalienable right to glean wherever she chooses. Instead, Ruth indicates another meaning for this phrase; she uses it as a sexual innuendo.[5] Ruth desires to glean, but also to use that gleaning as a forum for seducing a man to marry her. Of course, this is a long-term solution, and it will take time, but that seems to be no reason at all to delay the process. Ruth's mind is on marriage, and she will do whatever it takes to find that man.

Right after Ruth starts her gleaning, the scene shifts. The focus was on Ruth, but the narrative moves right past the sight of her gleaning in the fields to focus instead on Boaz, the rich, powerful owner of the field (Ruth 2:3–4). Boaz walks through his fields, greeting his workers along the way. The scene that follows is unmistakably sparse, and the narrative requires the reader's imagination to discover what is really happening. The vital action occurs just beyond the reader's scope of vision; one must watch the shadows to see what is going on.

> Then Boaz came from Bethlehem, and he said to the fieldworkers, "Yahweh be with you." They said to him, "May Yahweh bless you." Boaz said to his boy, who was in charge of the fieldworkers, "Who is this girl?" The boy who was in charge of the fieldworkers answered and said, "She is the Moabite girl who returned with Naomi from the country of Moab. She said, 'I wish to glean and to gather among the ears of grain after the fieldworkers,' and she came and stood from then in the morning until now. She stayed in the house only a little."
>
> Ruth 2:4–7

Boaz makes a beeline through his property and ends up in his own house. Once there, Boaz finds something he never expected. In his house are his chief servant, an overseer of the workers Boaz has already passed outside in the field, and an unknown foreign girl. The narrative never says what these two are doing, but we see plenty of circumstantial evidence. Ruth has already announced her intentions to seduce, and then we next find her in the landowner's house with a boy who struggles not to stutter as he tells his boss that she has only been there for a little while.

---

[5]Cp. Deuteronomy 24:1; Esther 2:15, 17.

One could easily get the notion that Ruth was well on the way to successful seduction. She had entered the field with a plan, and that plan involved both gleaning and seducing; she seems to have done both. Not only was her seduction working, but she was about to capture an overseer, someone much more worth her while than one of the other gleaners or one of the common fieldworkers. She strove to seduce a young gentleman in middle management, who had a future as well as a good enough job at present to support both her and Naomi.

Then the boss walks in and changes everything. On the one hand, Boaz' arrival ruins Ruth's affair with the overseer. Never again do we readers hear from that boy at all. He stutters in Boaz's face and then leaves the scene so quietly we hardly even notice the door swinging shut behind him. On the other hand, now Boaz begins to take an interest in Ruth. Her game changes entirely. No longer does Ruth play easy-to-get; she becomes a little aloof as she stoops to conquer this bigger prize. She even mouths off to Boaz: "you're treating me like one of your lowly servant-girls, and I am not like them at all" (Ruth 2:13). Throughout the rest of the harvest, Ruth suffices with her short-term solution, but she also keeps working toward the long-term solution of marriage to Boaz that could really take care of her and Naomi on a permanent basis.

Naomi also recognizes the potential. She encourages Ruth to stay around Boaz and not go chasing other men in other fields (Ruth 2:22). But Naomi adds something else to the whole picture. Boaz is a relative with potential to exercise the law of redemption. Naomi seems to hint that Ruth could seduce Boaz to exercise this power, providing a quick fix that might last. But Ruth does nothing for a while; her plans seem different.

The law of redemption was an unusual facet of ancient Israelite customs and codes. It envisioned a time when a family would have to sell all of its property in order to survive a particularly rough year. It seems that Elimelech sold off all of his property before he took Naomi and their two sons away from Israel. If Boaz would exercise the law of redemption, he would buy back that land from whomever owned it at the time, and would then give it to Naomi (as Elimelech's representative) at no charge.

But what could Naomi do with a piece of land? She and Ruth could not farm it together; that would be too much work for only two people. They had no money to hire laborers for the field. In Ruth's eyes, redemption was not an adequate long-term solution;

only marriage would ensure their future. So she waits to let her slow seduction work, but the harvest approaches an end, and Ruth's time was almost up before she took action again.

Boaz's Solutions

The action resumes once the barley and wheat harvests were at their end (Ruth 2:23). As long as there was some sort of harvest going on, Ruth and Naomi could survive by means of Ruth's gleaning, but the end of harvest was the sudden end of any short-term solution. Furthermore, Ruth seems obstructed by the circumstances. The narrative no longer depicts her as an instigator, as one who controls her own fate. Instead, Naomi takes the forefront once more.

To this point, the story has had two movements: the onset of crisis and Ruth's addition of roles. In response to famine and death, Ruth grows beyond her old roles of wife, daughter-in-law, and Moabitess to become husband, gleaner, and seducer. Now, the role additions become even more important, as other characters add roles themselves. This begins with Naomi, who takes the new role of matchmaker.

In Naomi's words, she desires to "seek a home" for Ruth. Once again, it is easy for the English reader to miss the point of this crucial statement. Naomi takes on a *father's* role of matchmaker. Fathers always arranged the marriages for their daughters.[6] Now Naomi goes beyond her old roles to take on a new social function. She selects a husband for Ruth and constructs the plans that will lead to the marriage. Naomi's tactics are seduction, just as Ruth's plan was. The difference now is Naomi's partnership in the process. Naomi joins Ruth in taking on new roles to overcome the crisis that has impacted both of them.

Next, Boaz begins to add roles, and at that point the story moves much more quickly. Boaz's initial role was as the receiver of Ruth's seduction; upon the threshing floor this role reaches its full realization (Ruth 3:8–9). Almost immediately, Boaz adds other roles. He becomes Ruth's suitor, responding appropriately to her role of seductress (Ruth 3:10–13). Then, he moves to his next role, which is the one that Naomi had desired for him. Boaz

---

[6]An instructive example is the search for Jacob's wife; though Rebekah instigates the search (Genesis 27:46), Isaac makes the arrangements (Genesis 28:1–5).

activates the law of redemption, and he takes the role of redeeming relative in a formal, legal sense (Ruth 4:1–6).

In the town square, Boaz locates the one relative who would have a prior claim to the purchase of Elimelech's property, and Boaz tricks this other relative into relinquishing the rights to the property. This allows Boaz to exercise the right of redemption, purchasing Elimelech's land as well as Ruth, the slave who was the property of Elimelech's estate. This would have provided a longer-term solution to Ruth and Naomi's problem, because it would have given their budget a large infusion of cash. Now they would have money to survive the winter, and perhaps through the next year, but redemption was no permanent solution at all.

Ruth's desired solution comes about next, as Boaz takes yet another role. He publicly offers to marry Ruth (Ruth 4:10). Though all of us modern readers know that this is a love story that ends with Boaz and Ruth marrying, the careful first reader would react with surprise at this revelation. Other close roles have been discussed before throughout the text, such as benefactor, lover, and redeemer, but never before has marriage entered into the picture. Ruth receives her highest hopes when Boaz adds the next role of husband.

After the marriage, Ruth has a son (Ruth 4:13–17). This son becomes Elimelech's legal heir, and thus the boy Obed is not truly Ruth's son; he is Naomi's son. For Naomi, the crisis began when she lost husband and sons; now, through the machinations of her surrogate "husband," Ruth, and Elimelech's legal stand-in, Boaz, Naomi receives her son, providing her with the solution that she has needed throughout the story. In this sense, the birth of the son and the recognition that this is truly *Naomi's* son is the climax and fulfillment of the whole narrative. Obed solves the problem.

The Problem's Dis-solution

But on another level, Obed is entirely secondary. The immense problems of Ruth and Naomi found their solutions not in the taking of the familiar roles of wife and mother, but in the dissolution of structures of expected action. Once everyone takes new roles, then the problem is solved. Ruth bears the child, but Naomi takes the role of mother. Ruth, the Moabitess, becomes worth more than seven sons. Obed is the son who is supposed to become the heir of great wealth, but his name sounds suspiciously like "slave." Boaz is now the man of this extended family, but he fades into the background. Boaz abdicates his right of naming the child, and instead gives that right to the women of the neighborhood, who are neither related nor male.

The start of the story features a family consisting of husband, wife, and two sons. Now, the family is grandmother and grandson (who have no direct genetic tie), along with an unrelated foreign daughter-in-law, an absent father, and the women of the neighborhood. Whatever else this story is, it is *not* a story idealizing the typical nuclear family. Such old-fashioned family structures bring only death in this story; the form of family that brings life is a sort of communal living among women with sons for slaves and men who show up only long enough to make babies.

In this sense, Obed does not solve the problem. Instead, the striving for a solution dis-solves the problem. In other words, when all the people in the story search for new roles, then the solution appears magically. The solution to the problem lies embedded in dissolution of society's structures that create women's poverty, among other problems. Ruth began by taking on new roles, including roles that violated the traditional definitions of gender behavior. As soon as this addition of roles spreads so that *everyone* takes on new roles of gender and social responsibility, the problem simply disappears. It dis-solves itself in a wholly new pattern of social existence.

Working Out Our Own Salvation

Another way of saying this is that this story's women work out their own salvation (Philippians 2:12). They search for ways to survive their lives with awe and uncertainty. God's presence somehow always evades their direct experience, but the divine possibilities for life explode around them as soon as they leave their old life behind them.

For them, salvation means the dissolution of traditional family values, because those values restrict them in ways that will lead soon to their death. Salvation also means the faith in their own ability to do new things. These women work in order to save themselves. Boaz may have had a sense of family responsibility, but Ruth and Naomi would have starved to death had they waited for Boaz to do something on his own. God may have intended their salvation, but they would never had found it had they stood still. For them, salvation means that Naomi gets a son, and Ruth is the savior by being surrogate son and then surrogate wife to produce that son. When these women take on such radically different roles, then they find the salvation toward which they have worked, and the result of this salvation is that all the women around them bless Yahweh (Ruth 4:14).

A Pilgrimage Toward Meaning

Looking for Meaning

The narrative structure of the story of Ruth depends upon the recognition of the characters' additions of new social roles. Ruth begins to take new roles, and then others do as well, until salvation comes in its glorious fullness. The spread of additional new roles possesses and expresses a saving power within this narrative. Once we readers discern this key to the plot, we can begin to look for meaning.

Perhaps the first way that we can make meaning out of this story is to emphasize that the women in the story are flexible, taking the social roles they must to achieve their goals. They are pragmatic. Ruth does what it takes to survive, and that means that she works to survive in a male world. She plays by the rules, and men make the rules. When we look at the story in this fashion, it is not a woman's world at all. It's a man's world through and through, and women must play by men's rules in order to survive.

If we press this far enough, then we can even say that women must become men in order to survive. Ruth becomes husband and the women of the community become father when they name Obed. Salvation only comes to women when they act like men. Maleness is normative; femaleness must change to match. Put this way, this meaning is quite distasteful and distressing, requiring us to search elsewhere for meaning. On the other hand, this does have a certain reality in patriarchal societies. In order to get ahead or even survive in cases when men do dominate, women often gain ground only by acting like men. This is a pragmatic meaning within this text, and should be valued as exactly that.

Looking Elsewhere for Meaning

Of course, it is also possible and valid to search elsewhere for the meaning of Ruth's story. Perhaps it is not the fact that this story's women act like men that is the crucial factor. Perhaps, instead, it is the willingness of *all* the story's characters to break down the barriers of social expectation. The women in the story are strong characters, full of their own intentions and plans, and they break social roles to affirm their selfhood. No one else tells them how to live. In fact, their very survival hinges upon their disregard for what the men think and what the powers of society decide should happen.

The point is even larger than that. Once women's violation of social roles spreads to men, all are saved. Ruth must act in ways that society says women shouldn't act. Naomi also takes a role that would be considered wrong for a woman. Boaz, too, does things that were outside the realm of propriety; he risks his own social acceptance to take on new social roles. For this reason, there are no victims and all are heroes in the course of the story. The women do *not* become the victims of male expectation; they *transform* male expectations in saving ways. This takes time and struggle, to be sure, but it brings the salvation of God into people's lives in concrete ways. Women begin the process, and women and men continue it together as they join in adding new and unexpected roles. The final product is the dissolution of social expectation.

Maleness and femaleness are both normative. Societal restrictions of roles are always arbitrary and thus never normative for God's people. The experience of salvation comes when people transcend the social restrictions and find God there, an ultimate reality beyond the boundaries of what we always thought had to be real.

It thus comes as no surprise that, in our search for meaning, we each take different roles. For that matter, those roles themselves must change as our journey continues. God is not within the boundaries of society; God is right past them, inviting us to new saving experiences of life.

Chapter 13

Esther

Esther is one of the two canonical books named after a woman; Ruth is the only other. Esther has another feature that sets it apart from other biblical books. This book never mentions God, either by the name of Yahweh or by any other title or attribute. God is strangely absent from the dealings of this plot and these characters. Instead, these characters work out their salvation on their own, even more so than was the case in the book of Ruth. Also, it is even more true that Esther, Mordecai, and the other Jews of this story work through their salvation with fear and trembling.

There is a sense in which Esther is a scary book. It takes place in Persia, the world's greatest power to date, under the reign of King Ahasuerus.[1] The issues appear in grand scale, and they are not pleasant issues suited for the squeamish of stomach or the faint of heart. There is capricious murder to start off this story, and soon treachery leads to full-scale genocide, prevented only by skillful manipulation of politics resulting in execution and the violent death of mass insurrection. The book is utterly serious; the issues are truly of life and death. All throughout, God stands at a distance and never appears at all on this story's stage of action, even though God seems to be waiting in the wings.

Within this context, the book of Esther presents two very different views of women. These two women control their sexual-

---

[1] Probably, Ahasuerus was the king better known as Xerxes, if there is any historical connection at all.

ity and use it to different ends. Both of these women are Persian queens, though there are very few similarities after that basic fact. Queen Vashti appears at the start of the story, but then Queen Esther takes over most of the narrative's attention.

Vashti, Queen of Persia

Vashti was the queen in the royal court of Persia.[2] Her husband was the king of Persia, Ahasuerus. Esther's first chapter narrates the scene for Vashti's execution in grandiose style. The story begins innocently enough, even if it does showcase an ostentatious display of wealth. Ahasuerus conducted a huge banquet in the third year of his reign. The king had set aside a full six months to show the inhabitants of the realm how rich and powerful he was. Then, he offered all of the people who lived in the capital, Susa, a banquet. The spread on the table was immense, and the banquet lasted a full week. The king's wealth was beyond almost any belief, and Ahasuerus intended to impress everyone with the size of his fortune. He spared no expense from this attempt to impress the whole world.

After a full week of feasting in the capital, the seven days of drinking too much wine had finally caught up with them. The king and his advisers had reached the point where the partying was the only thing on their minds, and suddenly the king had an idea. He would order the house servants to fetch Queen Vashti so that she could come and dance for their drunken dinner party. She was a beauty, and the king wanted to take a look. Moreover, he didn't seem to mind who else saw her beauty, either.[3] When she appeared for the king, then all the king's male friends could see how beautiful she was, and they would all know that the king's wealth was so great that it included even the most beautiful woman in the world.

Queen Vashti refused.

Vashti refused to go before the king when the king called to her. He was outraged. He asked his advisers what to do, and they

---

[2] For a more technical analysis of the court legends, including Esther, see Lawrence M. Wills, *The Jew in the Court of the Foreign King: Ancient Jewish Court Legends* (Harvard Dissertations in Religion; Minneapolis: Fortress Press, 1990).

[3] The book of Esther never makes the explicit claim that Ahasuerus asked Vashti to dance naked, though that very popular interpretation is certainly possible.

came up with a plan. The king would banish Vashti from his sight, never to see her again. Then, he would issue an imperial decree, to go throughout the nation and even throughout the known world that the Persians controlled. This decree would say that women had to obey men inside the house (Esther 2:22). Ahasuerus thought that this was a great idea.

The decree, of course, was ridiculous. It couldn't possibly change anything. The king's own household was the perfect example of how completely inept and ineffectual the law was; even the king could not make his wife, Queen Vashti, come or go as he pleased. Even after the law, she still stayed away, and he was deprived of the beauty that he had sought. With this law, nothing changed—except that the king lost something dear to him. No one gains, and the one who tries to gain loses.

Vashti also loses her rank and her privileges. It is unclear exactly what happens to her after this. Though she may have been put to death, it is quite likely that she was allowed to live in a secluded part of the imperial palace for the remainder of her days. She attempted to control her own sexuality and her own life, and she succeeded in asserting how she would act. However, there was a price for her defiance of the king. In gaining her pride, she lost many of her privileges; only she could say if the trade was worthwhile.

The entire scene with Vashti reads like a farce or a satire. The characterizations are obvious exaggerations, probably with some intention of comedy.[4] This mitigates the concerns we feel toward these events, because the intent of the story is to be crude, to go beyond sensible human actions into the laughable and the burlesque. But there is danger in this approach; it becomes far too easy to laugh off the real problems represented by Esther 1. If we see the story of Vashti as a satire, we must ask ourselves about the intended focus of the satiric critique. What are the assumptions behind this story? What are the foibles brought to light through the narrator's use of exaggeration?

With these questions, a better view of the Vashti story becomes possible. One of the issues that seems intended for criticism is the king's treatment of women. This issue arises first in a

---

[4]This notion of satirical comedy is developed in André LaCocque, *The Feminine Unconventional: Four Subversive Figures in Israel's Tradition* (Overtures to Biblical Theology 26; Minneapolis: Fortress Press, 1990), pp. 49–83, especially p. 51.

small comment right after the lengthy description of the king's lavish feast: "Queen Vashti also provided a feast for the women of the palace" (Esther 1:9). In the midst of all the opulence, the reader learns that the grandeur was only for the men. The women had another feast, but it receives so little attention that it seems to be a smaller, much less important occasion.[5] The king's treatment of Vashti is foolish; he only loses when he acts. By connecting the king's foolishness to the mistreatment of women as objects, the narrator argues that such treatment of women is, itself, folly. That viewpoint extends into Esther's story. When queens defy the king, the king's options are very limited, because any repression of a woman leads only to disaster for the king.

Though this does not excuse the text's humor at women's expense, at least it turns that humor back upon the men. Certainly, as the story progresses, it becomes impossible to laugh at the women, and some of the men receive the sharp sting of vicious irony. Still, Vashti's story is one of her unearned dishonor because of legitimate defiance, contrasted with men's greedy humor and clumsy attempts to force their own rule upon women.

Esther's Rise to Power

After Vashti's removal from the throne, Ahasuerus spent some time sulking, but then decided that he wanted sexual companionship once more. But no longer would there be a single queen who could attempt the kind of defiance at which Vashti had succeeded. Instead, Ahasuerus decided on a rotating harem on a grand, international scale. This king never does anything halfway. He decrees that officials be sent throughout the empire to search out eligible young beauties and bring them to the capital, Susa, where they would receive a year-long beauty treatment, perhaps also including some training in regal behavior (Esther 2:1–4, 12–14). At the end of the year's preparatory period, the young woman would be eligible for the king's attention. At any time that Ahasuerus desired female companionship, he would call for the next woman from the harem. After that one interaction, the woman would go to a second harem, where she

---

[5]Renita J. Weems, *Just a Sister Away: A Womanist Vision of Women's Relationships in the Bible* (San Diego, California: LuraMedia, 1988), pp. 100–101.

would live permanently unless the king was so impressed that he remembered her and called for her again by name.

This harem system was certainly well-organized. In this way, the king could receive maximum enjoyment from the young women of his empire without forming messy emotional attachments, such as the one with Vashti that had resulted in so much trouble. For most of these women, their one instance of sexual service for the king purchased them a comfortable existence for the rest of their lives.[6]

One night, in walks Esther.

The narrator has been careful to update us on Esther's whereabouts before this (Esther 2:5–11). Esther was one of the young rural Jewish women who became part of Ahasuerus' search for an enlarged harem. Furthermore, we readers have also learned about Esther's relatives. She was a Benjaminite, from the same tribe as Saul, Israel's first king. Esther's parents were either dead or separated from her by the exile, and so she was raised by her older cousin, Mordecai, who was a rising political adviser in the king's service. With the depth of detail given in the introduction, the narrative makes it clear that Esther and Mordecai will be the story's truly heroic protagonists. What remains, then, is for these heroes to meet with the king, in order to move toward the crux of the plot.

Ahasuerus falls in love with Esther at first sight. She thoroughly entrances him, and he soon forgets all of his vows of perpetual bachelorhood. He sends out for someone to bring him the crown that Vashti had once worn, but which had sat around in some dusty closet, forgotten. Ahasuerus places that crown on Esther's head and pronounces her as queen, not just for a night, but forever (Esther 2:17). With a great feast, the king introduces his new queen to the empire.

To this point, Esther's credentials are solely physical and sexual. Her attractiveness and memorable functioning in bed have made her queen. Her own control over her sexuality now extends to the king's, and it results in life—life for her in the court, in sharp contrast to Vashti's banishment from the palace. But the life and death are only beginning in this story; Esther's ability to

---

[6]Probably, it would be more correct to say that the guarantee lasted for the life of Ahasuerus. New kings were notorious for their disposal of prior harems. See 1 Samuel 30:3; 2 Samuel 3:7; 12:8–11; 16:21; and 1 Kings 20:5–7.

use control and sex to foster life over death will be sorely tested as this melodrama continues to unfold.

A precursor of the stakes of Esther's queenship appears immediately after the banquet. Mordecai overhears a plot to kill and overthrow King Ahasuerus, and he acts quickly upon those words. He tells Esther of the plot, and Esther passes on the information to the king. The ensuing investigation proves the truth of the words, and the conspirators feel the king's wrath as they hang to their death. Mordecai and Esther both rise in the king's esteem. Esther, it seems, is more than just a pretty face.

A Matter of Timing

Enter an enemy.

Haman was an Agagite, a member of the family that was traditionally the enemies of the Benjaminites, such as Esther and Mordecai.[7] Haman was an adviser to the king, and he was quite a high-ranking adviser at that. Most of the other king's servants were required to bow down to Haman to show their honor to the king's appointee, but Mordecai refuses (Esther 3:1–6). Of course, Mordecai's reasons were his devout Jewish piety that allowed such honor only to Yahweh, but that reason is never explained in the book of Esther; the name of Yahweh never appears at all.

Haman was egotistic; he could not stand Mordecai's failure to recognize publicly Haman's stature. Haman, in the stereotyping and caricaturizing typical of such melodramas, quickly jumps from his dislike of the individual, Mordecai, to a murderous intention of genocide against all Jews. Haman convinces his close friend and confidant, King Ahasuerus, to issue an irrevocable decree that would result in the death of all Jews (Esther 3:7–15). Of course, the text has told the readers repeatedly that Mordecai publicly admitted his Jewishness, but Esther kept her identity quiet (Esther 2:10, 20). Not even the king knows that his wife is a secret Jew, and that he has just ordered the murder of the queen.

The structure of the story's conflict now becomes crystal clear. Haman is the villain and Mordecai is the hero. They have already set themselves against each other. Esther, however, is an unknown: will she side with kin or with power? Likewise, the

---

[7]The roots of this antagonism are found in 1 Samuel 15.

king's alliances have yet to be discovered; we've been told that Ahasuerus is loyal to Haman, but what about Esther? Though the structure is now apparent, the crisis itself is only beginning.

Now that Haman and Mordecai have obligingly donned the overwrought garb of evil villain and courageous hero, they have become too stereotyped to carry the weight of the story. Though their warfare against each other will drive the plot, the real developments will occur elsewhere. Specifically, the chief question is Esther's loyalties. By claiming her ethnicity, her faith, and her very identity, she endangers life itself. Will she sell out her people to save herself? If she does serve her people, can she also keep her life, or will she become a martyr? But the questions run deeper. Can Esther influence Ahasuerus? Will her convictions be deep enough to change the king's mind? Will Esther's control of the situation be adequate for salvation?

These thematic questions walk right to the forefront of the text. Mordecai mourns the decree, and soon Esther asks him what's wrong. He explains the whole thing to her, working hard to enlist her in his cause.

> Mordecai warned Esther, "Don't think that you can escape this in the palace any more than all the other Jews. If you persist in silence this time, relief and deliverance will arise for Jews from somewhere else, but you and your family will perish. Who knows? Perhaps for a time like this did you come into the kingdom."
>
> Esther 4:13–14

Perhaps this is fate. Perhaps this moment is the whole reason Esther was born, and her entire life will hinge upon her actions in this one situation. Mordecai raises the stakes unbearably high, and so Esther agrees to risk her own life. For her to even approach the king without his prior request is to risk death, but she will face those chances.

Mordecai seems to express some sort of faith in divine intervention when he asserts that relief and deliverance will come from somewhere. But this faith is entirely within the human realm. God may work wonders of salvation on the earth, but always people provide the labor that makes those things happen. Mordecai's faith is practical; it provides motivation for action and places the responsibility squarely upon people. Yet the mystery is still present; if Esther will not perform the saving acts, someone else will. Perhaps it would be best to express Mordecai's belief as a faith in faith. He believes that if enough people have faith, then someone will do something that will work. In this book, salvation comes through human action.

Salvation Through Action

Esther hears Mordecai's lecture about proper action as the path to a practical salvation, but she doesn't seem to like what she hears at all. She recognizes her own need to take action, but it is still difficult to work against the established system, especially a system personified in evil figures such as Haman. Esther asks all of the Jews in the Persian capital to pray for her during a three-day fast (Esther 4:15–16). After that act of dedication and commitment, then she will go to the king and begin her task. She realizes full well the danger she faces: the king can deny her requests and can have her killed (Esther 4:16). After all, the new Queen Esther remembers quite well what happened to the former Queen Vashti.

Esther begins her plan with indirection. The story starts out in a straightforward manner. The readers know that Esther needs to ask a request of the king. She walks up to the king while he is sitting on his throne in the king's hall. This is precisely the right time, because the king is acting as king; he is taking care of official royal business. Esther approaches Ahasuerus, but she remains silent (Esther 5:2)! Though she knows exactly what she needs to ask, she does not say a thing. Then, the king asks her what she wants, and he promises to give everything to her, even if it is half of the whole kingdom. Once more, it seems that Esther has the perfect opportunity to make her petition of the king. If she just asks him to save the Jews, her difficult task will be completed once and for all. After all, Ahasuerus has just offered her anything she wants, and so he would give her this request. But Esther's plan is one of indirection. She passes by the opportunity to make a direct request; instead, she seeks to create a more delicate situation.

Esther invites the king and his servant, Haman, to a special private banquet that she will throw just for them later that day. The king hastens to fulfill this request, but he still knows that Esther has something else on her mind. While the three of them are drinking wine at the banquet, Ahasuerus once more asks Esther what she wants. Once more, she plays hard to get, and requests that the king and Haman come to another banquet the next day. At that meal, Esther will make known what she desires. Once more, the king agrees (Esther 5:6–9).

The contrasts come clear to the reader's eye. Esther, who must be active in order to give expression to her faith and to save her people, has become active only to a minimal degree. Her activity continues the process, but it is not decisive action. The king is eager to act, but that is because he does not understand the situation. Esther's special knowledge is still her advantage over Ahasuerus. With this knowledge, she chooses to take a path other than the direct one offered by the king. Because she knows more than the king, she takes an action that seems indirect to the readers. Esther's action is not decisive yet; she still seems to be setting the stage for the real action yet to come.

As the narrative continues, the plot shifts to focus on other characters. Esther disappears from the stage for the next twenty-four hours. Esther's absence lends as much to the action as her presence. Important things happen behind her back, and these new developments actually do set the the stage for the solution that does finally appear. Esther creates the time that allows the subsequent actions to happen, and those actions do provide the solution, but Esther does not *cause* this development herself. Of course, it may be that God provides the right coincidence of events, but the text itself never claims that. In fact, the story points to Esther's good timing as the cause of the solution. Because she allows the rest of the story to happen, she brings about success for her cause.

Even though Esther wins in the end, the story gets worse before it gets better. Immediately after the first banquet, Haman goes home to brag about his special privileged meal with the king and queen themselves. But on the way Haman sees Mordecai, and Mordecai still refuses to bow down. This enrages Haman more than ever before, and he rants and raves to his family and friends. "What good is all of my wealth and power," Haman fumes, "if that Jew doesn't bow down to me?" So Haman's wife, Zeresh, has a suggestion: build a gallows and ask Ahasuerus to hang Mordecai. Haman thinks it's a wonderful idea, and soon the gallows rise over the city, looming over the landscape.

Then the scene shifts once more. It is the dead of night in the palace, and the king can't sleep. He orders that some scribe read to him from the royal chronicles; perhaps the king wants exciting stories of the empire to regale him, or perhaps he is hoping for long lists of possessions that will surely lull him to sleep. For whatever reason, the reading happens upon that earlier story, when Mordecai overheard treason and passed the information along to Ahasuerus through Esther. Then a new thought occurs to the king. Nothing has ever been done to honor Mordecai, and, as the sun comes up to end a sleepless night, Ahasuerus decides that it is time to find some appropriate way to honor Mordecai in reward for his special service. As the king is thinking these thoughts, he receives an early-morning call, and he orders the visitor to enter.

In walks Haman, and immediately the king asks him, "What should I do for someone special?" Haman, of course, thinks only of himself, and describes a grand reward of wealth and prestige. Then the king orders Haman to perform this honor for Mordecai. Haman is crushed, and the story's cruel irony depicts Haman himself leading the procession to honor Mordecai throughout the city, and then slinking home afterwards in disgust and rage (Esther 6:1–11).

The main story picks back up after Haman's humiliation. It is now twenty-four eventful, sleepless hours after Esther's first banquet, and again she entertains Ahasuerus and Haman. Now, after Mordecai's elevation and Haman's new-found fear for his life, Esther makes her request. She asks the king to spare the life of her and her people (Esther 7:3–4). When the king hears this request, he is outraged that anyone would dare to plot such things against his beloved queen, and he demands her to tell him who had planned this evil deed. Esther quickly points at Haman and cries, "He did it!"

At this news, the king's fury knows no end, and so he arises in an uncontrollable anger that leaves him speechless. Not knowing what to say or do, he storms outside, trying to figure out his course of action.[8] Once the king exits, Haman begins to beg for his life. Thinking that he has no chance of mercy from the king, he prostrates himself on Esther's couch to plead with her. Then, Ahasuerus returns to Esther's room. When he sees Haman and Esther on the couch, the king suspects rape, and his accusation is as condemning as any judge's deliberated sentence. A nearby

---

[8]Again, there is clear contrast between the king and the queen. Esther knows what to do all along, but goes about it in an indirect fashion. Ahasuerus' anger prevents him from knowing a clear course, and so he wanders indeterminately until the situation changes and a plan of action is conspicuous.

servant adds another touch of irony by mentioning that the gallows, which Haman had built to be Mordecai's undoing, are near and available. Ahasuerus orders Haman to hang (Esther 7:1–10). Then, the king gives all of Haman's wealth to Esther and all of Haman's power to Mordecai, sealing the thorough reversal of fate.

With the story's enemy destroyed, the rest of the tale is anticlimactic, but nevertheless important. There is still the royal decree that all Jews be killed. Of course, royal decrees were inviolable; not even the king could change them after they had been issued. The king's word was the kind of law that even bound the lawgiver. The problem was too much for Ahasuerus, who never seems to be a man of deep thought. Instead, he gives his royal authority to Esther and Mordecai, promising to sign any-thing that they write (Esther 8:7–8). Together, they form a plan. Under the authority of the king, they send out a new decree, allowing the Jews throughout the Empire to defend themselves against the coming attack that would exterminate them. All in all, the Jews slaughter over seventy-five thousand Persians through-out the empire (Esther 9:6, 16). That is the true victory, accord-ing to this story. Through forceful action, the Jews bring about their own salvation, in response to the opportunity provided by the actions of Esther and Mordecai. So a big celebration follows, and then Mordecai commands all Jews to celebrate this feast through all time.[9]

A central theme within this narrative is Esther's taking advan-tage of opportunities. When situations arise that allow her to further her goals, she acts quickly and decisively. On the other hand, she is able to wait until the proper moment for action. In this story, timing is everything. In order to do the work of God, this woman refrains from action and then rushes into action, in the right proportion and direction, knowing when the time is right. Even though she cannot control the events of this male world, which is dominated by the unstoppable conflict between good Mordecai and evil Haman, she can operate within that world by noticing what happens and taking action that uses the

---

[9]Modern Jewish communities celebrate this feast, called Purim, in the spring. The joyous ceremony, involving the most raucous feasting of the entire Jewish liturgical year, centers on the reading of the story of Esther.

system to her own benefit. Likewise, no one can change the king's decree, but all of the Jews defend themselves and bring about their own survival.

We must note one other thing about our hero, Esther, at this point. Success is not enough for her or for the story. It is not enough that the Jews receive permission to live. They must also kill their enemies. It is not enough that the good Mordecai triumphs decisively over the evil Haman in obtaining the king's favor; Haman and all his ten sons must die humiliating deaths (Esther 7:10; 9:6–10, 14—15). Equality without redress is insufficient for Esther, just as is success without the utter removal of opposition and the structural change to accompany it.

Esther's Faith

In all the book of Esther, God is never mentioned. In many ways, this is a secular story of a religious woman who lives out her faith in the midst of the world, bringing about a worldly salvation for those whom she serves. Esther is a pious woman of faith, even though she takes no religious roles in the story. There are no options for her within the religion, because she is a woman. But there were open opportunities for her within the political realm of the court, and she took those opportunities and used them for all that they were worth. In the service of her goals, which were as religious as they were allowed to be, she did everything possible—and she succeeded.

The religious entities of her day allowed no opportunity for women to serve their God, and so Esther chose a way outside religion. Even though she worked outside the religion, she remained completely within her faith in God.

Esther provides a remarkable example of a woman struggling within the system of the male world. Caught between good and evil, she struggles to allow the good to triumph, despite all of the ways that the male-oriented world discriminated against her kind. She struggled, and she succeeded. Her victory was complete. In the context of the story's life and death battle, the tendency to take more gains than the minimum necessary to assure short-term survival seems quite understandable. Faced with the near threat of extermination, Esther and Mordecai choose to remove their enemies, so that the Jews can live not just for a while but for their entire future. Likewise in women's struggles, it becomes understandable to work not only for success in individual cases, but for the kind of widespread victory that allows improvement in women's lives for a long time to come. Such were Esther's effective actions, going well beyond the roles allowed to women in her time, but succeeding, because she was in the right place at the right time.

Chapter 14

A Few
More Stories

Ruth and Esther represent a very different type of story than that found earlier in the Old Testament. The stories of the Pentateuch and the historical narratives relate the tales of larger-than-life characters. Abraham's wealth is beyond imagination; Jacob's family life is outside most people's experience; Moses is closer to God than any human except perhaps one in a millennium or two. They are leaders of nations, kings equal to the emperors of the world's great powers in their power and fame. God comes to them in special ways to communicate the divine will to them alone.

These older stories were typical of the literature of their times, but Ruth and Esther depict a new tradition of Israel's stories. Ruth is an impoverished foreigner scratching out a living in Judah; Esther is a faithful Jewish orphan girl who finds herself part of the Persian Emperor's harem. Neither is born to advantage; no prophecies of glory accompany their births. Still, God works through them, and their stories take their rightful place alongside the older, grander stories.

Ruth and Esther's tradition of short stories represents God and humanity in a new way that complements the larger stories. The short stories emphasize human initiative and partnership with God. Correspondingly, God rarely enters these stories directly. In Moses' stories, it is not surprising to find divine intervention, such as the parting of the Red Sea in order to allow the Israelites to pass through on their way to safety and the promised land. But these short stories rarely show God in such a role. In fact, the book of Esther does not mention God at all. This does not mean that these short stories are any less religious than the older tales, but there seems to be a different concept of how God works in the world. God works exclusively through people in these short stories. At least, God's *visible* works are through human actions; if circumstances arrange themselves in just the right way to allow the story's progress, it may not be wrong at all to attribute the seeming coincidences to God's work, but the story never *shows* God's actions to the reader.

Because the short stories occur entirely within the human universe, they depict situations that are much closer to the real life happenings of modern people. Human faith becomes the crucial issue. Over and over again, we find the question: do these people have enough faith, or the right kind of faith, to do what is needed in the world? In other words, will religion suffice to allow the proper life in a complex world?

Certainly, the world of these short stories comes closer to our own world. These stories, mostly from the Persian period,[1] originate in a pluralistic time when the practice of Yahweh worship no longer controlled the state. In these two ways, their time was much like ours today. The wide variety of religious experience possible in our culture combines with an official separation between church and state to create a world in which many different ideas compete for attention and loyalty. Because there is no longer any official orthodoxy that the church or the government can enforce upon all, each individual must negotiate the divergent possible meanings offered by different systems of thought. Each event becomes susceptible to many meanings, as ascribed by different religions and philosophies. Certainty loses ground to the interplay of many thoughts. The risk of confusion is high, and these short stories reflect the conflict arising from the juxtaposition of different moral codes and religious commitments. But at the same time, individuals find the opportunity for deep commitment, because the cultural and religious plurality forces people to make decisions for one religion and against others. In the presence of such sincere, decisive commitments, new life for religion occurs out of the midst of plurality and confusion.

---

[1]Persia ruled the area around Jerusalem from 539 B.C.E. to 332 B.C.E. Certainly, at least some of these short stories come from the Hellenistic period right after that.

In the story of Ruth, God works through people who believe so much in life, in all of life's richness and possibilities, that they refuse to limit themselves to socially-defined roles. Once they begin to add new roles, they find solutions to their problems while creating a new way of life, fulfilling God's desires. In Esther's story, the characters' faith in the power of faith earns them the reward of survival. They take actions into their own hands because that is the way things have to be; God will work through people in the midst of a world with many competing ideas, to ensure the faith that has brought them to God. In these kinds of stories, there is room for women to act. God works through women as well as men, but it is not surprising to find women taking some of the most important roles within the short stories. These narratives present a practical faith that finds itself in action. The boundaries and restrictions of privilege that had dictated that God would speak only to men disappear when human action and faith become the crux of the stories. Women possess the same strength of faith and can undertake the same sorts of dynamic, effective actions for God; thus, they appear in these short stories with high frequency.

Though the Old Testament certainly contains many echoes of these ideas, the Pentateuchal stories of bigger-than-life heroes who meet personally with God and the historical narratives of kings who run nations in splendor and wealth became more normative than these more egalitarian stories. When the canon of the Bible was assembled, Torah and the prophets took pride of place, along with the other male heroes of faith. Stories of everyday life when God worked through people received much, much less attention. The number of popular short stories made it almost inevitable that a few would make it into the canon, and so Ruth and Esther took their places within the "official" parts of the tradition. Not surprisingly, the men who canonized scripture included mostly the stories about men. Other stories about women were excluded from scripture.

Even though Ruth and Esther are well-known tales from the Old Testament itself, there are a few more short stories that deserve attention. These narratives did not make it into the canon, but ancient Jews respected these stories in much the same way that they did the stories of Ruth and Esther. Several Christian traditions still include these additional stories in their canon, though Protestant Christians place them in the Apocrypha. Nevertheless, the stories of Judith and Susanna uphold the value of women and women's faith.

Judith

Esther's story was full of indirection, but Judith outdoes even Esther in the story's ability to postpone the solution. Judith herself does not appear until halfway through the book! The story begins with a lengthy, complex description of international politics, though the names of the imperial leaders do not correspond to the known historical conditions.[2] Nebuchadnezzar is the evil king in this story, and even though the historical Nebuchadnezzar was the king of Babylonia, this Nebuchadnezzar was the king of Assyria, the very kingdom later conquered by Babylonia. Nebuchadnezzar hired for himself a military general to prosecute Nebuchadnezzar's evil intentions, and this general's name was Holofernes.

Nebuchadnezzar and Holofernes embarked upon a massive military campaign, designed on a scale that surprised the whole world. Their army was beyond number as they marched west, taking one country after another. Soon, nations in their path feared for their life, and so they sued for peace, offering to pay tribute, to allow the destruction of their gods, and to worship Nebuchadnezzar alone, all in exchange for their safety from the advancing army. In the celebration of such easy victory, the army rested for a month to replenish its supplies, right on the border of Judah.

Soon, the word reached the Jews, who had returned from exile not long before and so still had a very healthy respect and fear for such large imperial armies. In response, the Jerusalem leadership ordered the men of the small town of Bethulia to occupy and defend the mountain passes, thus blocking access to the rest of Judah. With sackcloth, fasting, and prayer, the Israelites entreated God to save them from this Gentile horde.

---

[2]André LaCocque, *The Feminine Unconventional: Four Subversive Figures in Israel's Tradition* (Overtures to Biblical Theology 26; Minneapolis: Fortress Press, 1990), pp. 31–32, argues that the book of Judith exhibits "intentional historical and geographical blunders," thus creating a clear sense of fiction.

Holofernes, on the other hand, did not care for such religious preparations, but he heard reports of the Jews' military movements to the mountain passes. Holofernes consulted an adviser, Achior, to find out about these Jews. Achior recounted the grand story of Jewish history from Abraham to the return from exile, and he summarized the connection of religion to history for the Jews: "If the Jews have sinned, we can conquer them; if they have been pure, then they will make fools out of us" (cp. Judith 5:20–21). Not only is this a life and death issue for the Jews, but it is also a test of faith, and the story of Judith seems to claim even that the test of faith is the *primary* event.

Holofernes found Achior's answer not only inappropriate, but even treasonous, and the army cast out Achior in disgust and anger. But some Jews found Achior, and used him as an opportunity to discover Nebuchadnezzar's sinister plans to destroy them. In this case, however, there was no way for the Jews to use this inside information to their benefit. Soon, Nebuchadnezzar and Holofernes placed Bethulia under siege with their massive armies, and in just over a month, the water was gone. Bethulia was faced with death by thirst. The city went into despair, and they were ready to surrender to Holofernes, even though they knew that they would lose everything. But they decided to give God five days to do something before they surrendered. Their salvation would have to come soon, or else it would be too late. Up to this point, the story has offered sinister heroes like Nebuchadnezzar and Holofernes, and a few more neutral characters such as Achior, but there have been no heroes, no one who could effectively bring God's salvation to the people of faith in the hours of final need.

Then Judith entered.

Judith was a widow in Bethulia whose wealthy husband had died over three years before of heat stroke. She was prosperous herself, since her husband had left her with plenty of property and servants, and she was well respected, since she was virtuous and pious. Judith had heard the plans to surrender in five days, and she became outraged. In a long speech (Judith 8:11–27), she expressed her faith, claiming that all of the citizens of Bethulia should set an example for all Jews through their faithful action. They should die in defense of their land rather than submit to slavery and the worship of pagan gods; for Judith, surrender was not an option for consideration at all. Her faith required action, and she had faith that God would respond to action and that action would engender even more action, until salvation was reached.

The Israelites recognized the propriety of Judith's faithful piety, but the pain of their present situation was all that they could see. One of them told Judith to pray for rain, since she was so pious, but instead she responded that she would soon do something that would become famous throughout the generations.

Judith's following course of activity represents an important paradigm for women's creative and courageous action even today. She begins with prayer (Judith 9:2–14); her subsequent actions are firmly grounded in the piety of personal relationship with God and in the certain knowledge of faith. Her prayer retells history, focusing on the story of Dinah. She knows the scriptural stories and can apply them to her own situation. Further, her prayer indicates a solid grasp of the true international condition, which she sees in the perspective of God's own presence and activity in the world. God's might and effectiveness do not depend upon the powers of humans nor their numbers (Judith 9:11); God's active presence in the world is of a different character altogether. Nebuchadnezzar cannot compete, despite the vast numbers of his armies, because he and God are in completely different categories. Throughout this prayer, Judith orients herself to the service of God. She desires what God desires for the world. She works for the fulfillment of God's purposes, and she strives to bring God's praise into the world. This prayer determines Judith's purpose and thus sets the course for her effective action.

Once the prayer was over, Judith set to work. She dressed herself in her most attractive fashion, and then walked right out of the city gates and into the patrols of the army besieging Bethulia. Once captured, she claimed that she was an intentional defector, looking for Holofernes so that she could give him crucial information that would speed his victory. Even though Bethulia could do nothing with secret information, Holofernes' army was massive and could take advantage of military intelligence. They took her to the general, and she explained to him her plan. She would pray to God outside the camp every night, and God would tell her when Bethulia had sinned. Then she would pass that knowledge to Holofernes. When all the Jews sinned, God would forsake them and then the armies of Nebuchadnezzar could take an easy victory over them (Judith 11:17). Holofernes accepted the plan, complimenting both her beauty and her wisdom.

Beauty and wisdom combined to bring about Holofernes' downfall. Because of Judith's wisdom, she insinuated herself regularly into the general's presence by means of this deceit. Through her beauty, she accomplished seduction. Holofernes asked Judith to a banquet that quickly became a private drinking bout (Judith 12:13–20). Late that night, after Holofernes passed out from excessive alcohol, Judith took his sword and beheaded him (Judith 13:6–8). She put his head in her foodbag, and then she walked right out of the camp and right back into Bethulia, where she presented the elders of her city with the severed head of their enemy. The armies reacted with severe panic; one could say that they too lost their heads. The men of Bethulia chased the fleeing armies and slaughtered them on the run. The siege was over, and their salvation had come to them in a woman's foodbag.

Judith concluded the tale with a hymn of praise, just as she began her action with prayer. Judith then gave large offerings to the service of God, and she grew in her piety. She remained a widow throughout her long life, and she became truly famous.

Judith's story is a true adventure tale. She uses every means at her disposal to defeat a horrendous enemy, and she retains her virtue at every point along the way. She presents a very active role model for women of faith. She decides what must be done and then she does it, at any cost. She holds her head high when she walks out of Bethulia and also when she walks back inside her home city's gates. She earns respect, and she can compete with any man and prove herself his superior, not just his equal. No task is too difficult or too unpleasant for her; she does what the situation requires. Furthermore, she undertakes these worldly tasks with her faith firmly grasped in her mind. She acts because of faith and because of God's reality in her life. She is a defender of the faith in every sense. Faith motivates Judith to undertake bold, decisive actions. Because of those faithful actions, she gains the respect of her community, women and men alike, as they realize her abilities and her commitments.

Susanna

The next story represents a different model of women's faith. In this very short story, women's beauty and men's wisdom are the problems and piety is the solution.

Susanna was the wife of Joakim, a rich man whose wisdom was well-known throughout the local Jews. Two Jewish elders used to frequent Joakim's property while they were seeking his counsel in decision-making, and they often saw Susanna. These elders were attracted to the area by Joakim's wisdom, but once there they lusted after Susanna's great beauty. Of course, each elder never mentioned his lust to the other; both desperately desired to preserve appearances.

Once when these elders were both at Joakim's, they agreed to part for lunch, but both of them doubled back to hide in the bushes and peer at Susanna. They ran into each other, and with embarrassment, they admitted to each other that they lusted for Susanna (Susanna 13–14). In that moment, they transformed themselves from hypocrites who had tried to hide their sin from each other to conniving degenerates whose sins prodded each of them to greater sin. They hatched their plot and sought for the right time to betray their victim.

The opportunity came in the garden, when Susanna bathed alone. The elders approached her and explained the situation that they had contrived. No one could come help Susanna; she was alone. If she consented to sex with each of the elders, then they would not harm her otherwise, but if she refused, then they would condemn her with a charge of adultery with some young man. The witness of two elders would legally confirm the accused adultery, and the penalty would be Susanna's death. Though there seems to be no physical force here, the result is the same as rape: Susanna must choose between unwanted sex and death. Susanna's response is quick and clear, recognizing the trap: "I will let you kill me rather than sin" (Susanna 23).[3] Her piety moves her to purity, at any cost.

At the trial, Susanna cries out to God for help, and Daniel arrives. He offers his assistance in the legal proceedings, and he asks to interrogate each of the elders separately. Daniel asks

---

[3]A word of caution is most needed; we must not fall into the trap set here for interpreters. The point of Susanna's response is protest. Had she been victimized by rape, that would not have been sin for her. Women's experience of being raped is not sin. Susanna, though, had a real choice (as her eventual salvation attests within the narrative's logic) and thus her participation would not have been rape, but adultery according to the customary law. Within this context, Susanna had a real choice, and her right decision drives the story to its conclusion where events prove the rightness of her choice. But this does *not* speak to the rightness of modern rape victims' resistance.

each to identify the tree under which they caught Susanna in adultery. When they disagree with each other, Daniel kills both of the elders. This saves and vindicates Susanna, and also establishes a reputation for Daniel.[4]

The elders' mistake came much earlier in the story, really. They thought that Susanna had only two choices: sex or death. But she had another option: legal protest. Susanna's salvation begins when she has faith in the Jewish faith, including its legal system. She risks even her life on her faith and on her belief that God would make some salvation possible, through some means. As in many of these short stories, faith in the faithful actions of others brings salvation.

Susanna is a mostly passive figure. She makes two choices and two statements, first when she denies the elders and second when she protests during the trial. Her statements are both protests, and in this sense she is powerful and active, holding to her faith in God despite the evils of men. Her faithful protests trigger salvation, but then she waits for God's instruments of salvation to come to her, in the form of Daniel.

In contrast, Judith is entirely active. Once she hears what has happened, she takes immediate action. Prayer and praise frame her deed, but the deed itself is central and it is extremely decisive: deceit, seduction, and decapitation. She brings salvation to all her people in Bethulia through that action.

Together, Susanna and Judith provide a pair of possible women's responses. Judith brings death; Susanna faces the chance of her own death. Judith takes action using her wisdom and beauty; Susanna relies only on her faith. Both the more active example of Judith and the less active model of Susanna lead to the arrival of God's salvation, transmitted to the human realm by the actions of these women. Neither violent action nor passivity are wrong choices for women of faith; God responds to both and joins with both styles in faithful partnership that effects salvation.

---

[4]In the Greek version of the Bible, the story of Susanna appears as part of the book of Daniel.

Chapter **15**

The Next
Stories

Throughout this study, we have discovered women's stories of faith from the earliest chapters of Genesis to some of the latest stories of the Protestant Old Testament. We have even seen how other women's stories from ancient Israel are present in the larger canon used by Catholic and Orthodox traditions. But the stories of women's faith do not end there. The New Testament tells other stories, and church history records the tales of many other women. Beyond that, these stories echo in the lives of women today who seek to find and to express their faith in accord with their lives as women.

Women's Faith

We have heard a wide variety of stories. In the Old Testament and the Apocrypha, women's faith comes in many different shapes and styles. Faith expresses itself through many situations amid women in all walks of life. The wide variety of these stories teaches us an important point. There is no one kind of women's faith or women's experience. There is no one small set of roles for women's faith. There is no limit at all to women's faith, even though society keeps trying to put women within stringently defined boundaries.

The story of Old Testament faith begins in the early days, when women were almost equal with men in their tasks and functions. In these years of early Israel, women and men worked together to scratch out a bare living among the rocky hillsides of Canaan. Israelites rejected the tyranny of the cities and instead flourished among those hills, where they could live together as equals in Yahweh's sight. But as time went on, there was an increasing need to maximize the population for sheer survival, and this resulted in a group of temporary laws that shifted women's attentions from the tasks they shared with men to the one task they alone could do: childbearing. Women lost more and more of the general functions as this happened, and they also lost status. Specialization became marginalization.

The story of Eve was one of the stories told as the monarchy began. In those days, urbanization further lessened women's rights and roles. The story of Eve shows a strong woman whom God commands to labor *both* in the field and in childbirth. But this social movement failed in its opposition to the limitation of women's roles. Soon, the literature depicts only silent women, such as Sarah, Hagar, and Sarah's niece. These women suffer without even the opportunity to give voice to their pain. Rebekah's voice appears briefly, and we are once more entranced at a voice that can solve problems and bring life's fullness. But those women's voices are so rarely heard at all. Even worse, men treat women as objects to be bought and sold, as happened to Rachel, Leah, and Dinah. As objects, they often become victims, and then they even take the blame for their own victimization. The cycle that began with role limitation and silence results in harsh intensification of women's pain. Some women take charge of their own lives, and though these are often painful stories (as in the case of Potiphar's wife and Tamar, Judah's daughter-in-law), there is still the hope of solution to the many problems plaguing women, the problems that began when men limited women's roles.

Nevertheless, it is possible for women to proclaim their faith, as did Miriam and Rahab. These women used power in helpful, beneficial ways to spread faith and to increase life, even though they each suffered because of their choices of active, helping roles. Women could use power effectively for good causes, as Deborah and Jael did, though characters like Delilah corrupted power. In Judges, Jephthah's daughter found the power of community, but the Levite's concubine experienced only the powerlessness of dismemberment and dispersion.

The monarchy allowed few roles for women. The wives within the royal court were often treated as if they were only objects, but

Bathsheba was able to rise above the situation to exercise power as queen-mother. The prophets, working later within the monarchy, found women to be powerful symbols for what could go wrong with men's lives, further degrading the status of women.

Later in Israel's history, some more hopeful notes were added to the tune of women's faith. The scribal wisdom tradition produced a portrait of Lady Wisdom, who was God's partner in creation. Then came the short stories about women of faith who acted within the world to bring about the salvation of themselves and others. Ruth added more roles to her repertoire of action, including men's roles, until everyone in the story started breaking down the social boundaries of expectation. Once that happened, all received the salvation for which they sought. Esther was more effective in the political realm, working behind the scenes of international politics to bring about the Jews' salvation from a death sentence. Judith brought military victory to her people when they were at the edge of death, whereas Susanna succeeded in salvation on a more personal level of piety.

All of these stories show ways that women can act within the world and within faith. There were many ways in which women were victimized, but there were also many opportunities for women to save and to serve God's intentions. Both are possible; both happen regularly. These stories show us the range of reality, helping us to face the events around us with open eyes.

Telling the Truth in Love

These stories empower us. When we know these women's stories, then we can tell them. In telling these stories of faith, there is the possibility for newness. We can realize just how much the ancient stories are like our stories; these ancient women can show us ourselves and our modern world in great clarity.

These stories are true. They express life the way it was and the way it is. Of course, many of the details of these stories may have been embellished or derived, but the stories strive to talk about true human experience, and especially true experiences of women. When we tell these stories, we tell the truth, and it is of the utmost importance for women of every generation that we tell the truth.

The truth about women contains wonderfully good news and also terrifying tales. There are horrible stories in the Old Testament about women's suppression and oppression. Women were disallowed many of the common rights and privileges of life. They were threatened by disease and death and by the men in their lives. The stories show us in no uncertain terms how bad life can be for women. Women's lives were forfeited over and over again by the very men who claimed to love them. Men's desire for power resulted too often in the degradation and abandonment of women. Men's desire for control produced restrictions on women's expression and livelihood that left women on the very margins of that society, frequently without the means for adequate livelihoods. The truth about women includes their mistreatment.

We may want to hide from these stories. They are unpleasant in the extreme; they raise issues we may wish to avoid or deny. The stories are full of murder, betrayal, rape, and mutilation. But these stories tell the truth. They speak of life as it really was for women and as it often is today for women who still live in an abusive, male world. These stories speak the truth and thus bring the light of day into the darkened corners of our society, uncovering the sins that still permeate our lives.

But the truth is not all bad, either. These stories tell about women's leadership and women's proclamation of their faith. There have always been women who transcend the boundaries that their society places upon them. There have always been women whose faith motivates them to acts of courage and to powerful ministries that make faith known and felt. These stories speak the truth that society can never hold down all women, and that women can and should be effective servants of God, in the full range of roles that society provides for men in their service. Women in the Old Testament are preachers, proclaimers, wealthy and powerful supporters, prophets, military heroes, and judges. These ancient women of faith are also commoners, average people with normal lives who find ways to serve God in the everyday facets of their lives. Women's faith is for rich and poor alike, for weak and powerful, for urban and rural women, for pacifists and activists, for oppressed and advantaged alike.

These stories speak truth to us. They tell us how horrible life can be for some women. In a world so quick to deny pain, in a religion too hasty to sweep such evil under the rug and to ignore that bad things happen to modern women, we need the truth of these stories, because only this kind of shocking truth can empower action and comfort. These stories also tell us about the power of faith to transform the lives of all women, and about the roles available to women to express that faith. In a society that still limits what things are deemed "appropriate" for women, especially within the confines of the church and its bureaucratic structures of ministry, we greatly need to speak the truth about women's potential for service in all possible roles. For both good and bad, we need these stories to speak the truth about the ancient women of faith, because the point of the story is just as true today.

Making Choices

The effects of these stories begin in speaking the truth about the past, and we can quickly observe that it is also the truth about the present. But the effects do not stop there. These stories also begin to shape the future.

There are choices to be made. The church as a whole must choose how to treat women inside and outside the church. Will women truly be included as full participants in our churches? Will the full range of roles be opened? These stories can help us make such choices in the right direction, as we see how God's ancient women took successful roles in the experience and propagation of faith. On an individual level, there are also choices. Will a certain woman realize her God-given potential and receive the empowerment to answer her call through work in the world? Will a certain man pursue the power that the society provides him in ways that injure women? These stories make plain the pains and joys of such choices, and they depict God's desires within human conduct in clear ways.

Crucial issues are at stake. Will we lapse into the stifling silences? Will we champion the oppression of women by calling it "God's will"? Will more women die from abuse and evil pursuit of power? Will God's intentions for creation manifest themselves by enabling women to achieve and receive their God-given potential?

God intends a life for all women that includes them fully within the communities of faith, just as God intends the same thing for all men. In God's vision of the world, women and men live together in peace and harmony, without the dangerous hierarchies that dismantle creation in order to build edifices to power and ego. In God's vision, the atrocities never occur again, and women rise to lead themselves and men into new relationships with each other and with God.

The story ends as it starts, which makes sense, because the story began at its ending. The end—the goal—of women's faith is the attainment of God's vision for the whole world. We end the stories by living them out, just as we began the stories while searching for ways to live in this precarious world. Through the stories, we may come closer—at least a little bit closer—to finding paths to God's vision.

May God's vision come. May it hasten into our world as we hear the distant, vibrant echoes of these stories of women's ancient faith. May we do our part to bring this vision to reality.

Index of Biblical Names

Index of Scripture References

Made in the USA
Las Vegas, NV
24 November 2023

81412099R00111